INTRO TO COMPUTER SCIENCE

A Coding Primer with Python and Java

THOMPSON CARTER

TABLE OF CONTENTS

INTRODUCTION

Intro to Computer Science: A Coding Primer with Python and Java

In an increasingly digital world, the ability to understand and write computer code is not just a valuable skill but a critical one. Programming has transcended its origins as a niche activity for computer scientists and has become a cornerstone of modern education, business, and innovation. Whether you're looking to embark on a career in technology, enhance your problem-solving abilities, or simply explore the fascinating world of computers, this book provides a structured and approachable guide to mastering the fundamentals of computer science through hands-on programming in Python and Java.

The Purpose of This Book

This book, ***Intro to Computer Science: A Coding Primer with Python and Java***, is designed for beginners eager to dive into the world of coding and computer science. Unlike many technical books, which can overwhelm new learners with jargon and theoretical concepts, this book adopts a jargon-free, practical approach. It focuses on real-world examples and hands-on exercises to ensure that you not only understand the concepts but also learn how to apply them in practical scenarios.

By the end of this book, you'll have a solid foundation in the principles of computer science, a working knowledge of two of the most popular programming languages, Python and Java, and the confidence to tackle real-world problems with code.

Why Learn Computer Science?

Computer science is the driving force behind the technology we use daily. From social media and online shopping to artificial intelligence and medical advancements, computer science underpins almost every modern innovation. Understanding its principles and applications is empowering, offering you the ability to:

- **Solve Real-World Problems**: Develop solutions for challenges in healthcare, finance, education, and more.
- **Enhance Career Opportunities**: Enter the tech industry or enhance your existing career with technical skills.
- **Foster Creativity**: Design games, applications, and digital tools to bring your ideas to life.
- **Develop Logical Thinking**: Strengthen your ability to think systematically and solve problems efficiently.

Whether you're a student, a working professional, or simply a curious learner, understanding computer science can unlock countless opportunities and help you navigate an increasingly technology-driven world.

Why Python and Java?

This book focuses on **Python** and **Java** because these languages represent two distinct yet complementary paradigms in programming.

1. **Python**:
   - **Simplicity**: Python's clean and readable syntax makes it ideal for beginners.
   - **Versatility**: Widely used in data analysis, artificial intelligence, web development, and automation.
   - **Popularity**: Python consistently ranks as one of the top programming languages globally.
2. **Java**:
   - **Robustness**: Known for its strong type system and extensive libraries.
   - **Platform Independence**: "Write once, run anywhere" thanks to the Java Virtual Machine (JVM).
   - **Enterprise Applications**: A leading choice for large-scale, high-performance systems.

By learning both languages, you'll gain a well-rounded understanding of programming and prepare yourself for

CHAPTER 1: INTRODUCTION TO COMPUTER SCIENCE

Computer science is a dynamic and ever-evolving field that powers nearly every aspect of modern life. From the smartphones in our hands to the algorithms that recommend our next favorite movie, computer science is the foundation of the digital age. This chapter explores what computer science is, its core areas, and how it drives the technologies we rely on daily.

1.1 What is Computer Science?

At its core, computer science is the study of computers and computational systems. It encompasses:

- **Theoretical Foundations**:
  - How information is represented, processed, and communicated.
- **Practical Applications**:
  - Developing algorithms, software, and systems to solve real-world problems.

Computer science is not just about programming—it's about understanding problems, designing solutions, and implementing them effectively. It combines logical reasoning, creativity, and technical skills to create systems that improve lives, automate processes, and solve complex challenges.

1.1.1 The Role of Computers

Computers are tools that execute instructions to process data. Computer science focuses on making these instructions (software) efficient, reliable, and scalable to handle diverse tasks, such as:

- Storing and retrieving data (e.g., databases).
- Analyzing patterns (e.g., machine learning).
- Communicating across networks (e.g., the internet).

1.2 Key Fields in Computer Science

Computer science spans several domains, each with its unique challenges and applications. Here are four foundational fields:

1.2.1 Algorithms

An **algorithm** is a step-by-step procedure for solving a problem or performing a task. Algorithms form the backbone of computer science by defining how data is processed.

Examples:

- Sorting algorithms, like quicksort, for organizing data.
- Search algorithms, like binary search, for finding information quickly.

Real-World Impact:

- E-commerce platforms like Amazon use algorithms to sort products and recommend items.
- GPS systems calculate the fastest route using pathfinding algorithms.

1.2.2 Data Structures

Data structures are ways of organizing and storing data so it can be accessed and modified efficiently. They include:

- Arrays, linked lists, stacks, queues.
- More complex structures like trees, graphs, and hash tables.

Real-World Impact:

- Social networks like Facebook use graph structures to model relationships between users.
- Databases store and retrieve structured data using optimized data structures.

1.2.3 Networking

Networking focuses on how computers communicate with each other to share information. It involves:

- Protocols like HTTP (web), FTP (file transfer), and TCP/IP (core internet protocols).
- Infrastructure like servers, routers, and cloud systems.

Real-World Impact:

- Video conferencing platforms like Zoom rely on networking protocols to transmit audio and video data in real time.
- Online gaming connects players globally through robust network architectures.

1.2.4 Artificial Intelligence (AI)

AI enables machines to mimic human intelligence by learning from data, recognizing patterns, and making decisions.

Examples:

- Machine learning for predictive analytics.
- Natural language processing for chatbots like ChatGPT.
- Computer vision for self-driving cars.

Real-World Impact:

- AI powers personalized recommendations on platforms like Netflix and Spotify.
- It helps in medical diagnostics, identifying diseases from scans.

1.3 Real-World Examples: How Computer Science Powers Modern Applications

Computer science innovations have revolutionized industries and shaped how we live. Let's examine a few examples:

1.3.1 E-Commerce

- Algorithms analyze user behavior to recommend products, optimize pricing, and streamline logistics.
- Data structures store millions of products and user records, ensuring fast and reliable searches.

1.3.2 Social Media

- Networking allows instant communication across continents.
- AI filters content, recommends friends, and detects harmful behavior.

1.3.3 Healthcare

- AI assists in diagnosing diseases, predicting patient outcomes, and personalizing treatment plans.
- Data structures manage massive medical records efficiently.

1.3.4 Entertainment

- Streaming platforms like YouTube and Netflix use algorithms to suggest content tailored to user preferences.
- Networking ensures videos load quickly, even during peak usage.

1.4 Why Learn Computer Science?

Understanding computer science equips you with skills that are highly sought after in today's technology-driven world. It allows you to:

- Solve real-world problems efficiently.
- Automate repetitive tasks and improve productivity.
- Build systems that impact millions of lives, from mobile apps to large-scale platforms.

Moreover, computer science fosters critical thinking, logical reasoning, and creativity—skills that are valuable across industries.

Computer science is a versatile and impactful discipline that combines theory, practical application, and creativity. Its core fields—algorithms, data structures, networking, and AI—form the foundation for developing technologies that power modern life. By learning computer science, you're not just acquiring technical skills; you're gaining the tools to shape the future.

In the next chapter, we'll explore programming basics, introducing you to how computers interpret instructions and how we can harness programming languages to create meaningful solutions.

CHAPTER 2: PROGRAMMING BASICS

Programming is at the heart of computer science. It's how we communicate with computers, instructing them to perform specific tasks efficiently and accurately. Whether it's building software, automating processes, or analyzing data, programming serves as the tool that brings our ideas to life. In this chapter, we'll demystify what programming is, trace the evolution of programming languages, and use a relatable analogy to explain how programming works.

2.1 What is Programming? Understanding Code as Instructions

At its simplest, **programming** is the process of writing instructions for a computer to execute. These instructions, called **code**, are written in specific languages that computers understand.

2.1.1 Why Do We Need Programming?

Computers are powerful machines capable of performing billions of calculations per second, but they are fundamentally dumb—they can only do what we tell them to do. Programming bridges this gap by:

- **Defining tasks**: Telling the computer exactly what to do.
- **Automating processes**: Eliminating repetitive manual work.
- **Solving problems**: Providing tools to analyze, compute, and create solutions.

Example:

- Writing a program to calculate the average of a list of numbers. Without programming, this task would need to be done manually for every new list.

2.1.2 How Do Computers Understand Code?

1. **Binary Language**:
   - At the hardware level, computers only understand binary (1s and 0s).
   - Every operation—from displaying text to playing music—translates into sequences of binary instructions.
2. **Programming Languages**:

- o To make programming more human-friendly, we use higher-level languages like Python and Java.
- o These languages are translated into machine-readable binary through tools like **compilers** (for Java) or **interpreters** (for Python).

2.1.3 Example of Code in Action

Here's a simple Python program to add two numbers:

python

```
num1 = 5
num2 = 10
result = num1 + num2
print("The sum is:", result)
```

What Happens:

1. The program stores 5 in num1 and 10 in num2.
2. It adds the two numbers and stores the result.
3. It displays the result to the user.

2.2 The Evolution of Programming Languages

Programming has come a long way since the early days of computers. Here's a brief timeline of its evolution:

2.2.1 First-Generation Languages: Machine Code

- **Description**: Binary code directly executed by the CPU.
- **Characteristics**:
    - Extremely fast but hard to write and debug.
    - Example: 10110000 01100001 (an instruction to move data).
- **Usage**: Used in the earliest computers.

2.2.2 Second-Generation Languages: Assembly Language

- **Description**: Symbolic representation of machine code.
- **Characteristics**:
    - Easier to understand than binary.
    - Requires an **assembler** to convert it into machine code.
- **Example**: MOV A, 61H (move value into register A).
- **Usage**: System programming for hardware-level tasks.

2.2.3 Third-Generation Languages: High-Level Languages

- **Description**: Human-readable languages like Python, Java, and C.
- **Characteristics**:
    - Abstract away hardware complexities.

- o Use compilers or interpreters to translate into machine code.
- **Examples**:
  - o Python: print("Hello, World!")
  - o Java: System.out.println("Hello, World!");
- **Usage**: Web development, data analysis, application development.

2.2.4 Fourth-Generation and Beyond

- **Fourth-Generation Languages (4GL)**:
  - o Designed for specific tasks like database querying.
  - o Example: SQL (SELECT * FROM users;).
- **Fifth-Generation Languages (5GL)**:
  - o Focused on solving problems using constraints and logic.
  - o Example: Prolog, used in AI.

2.2.5 The Shift to Python and Java

Python and Java have emerged as two of the most popular languages for beginners and professionals alike because of:

- **Python**:
  - o Easy syntax and readability.

- Extensive libraries for automation, data science, and web development.
- **Java**:
  - Platform independence through the Java Virtual Machine (JVM).
  - Strong typing for robust, enterprise-grade applications.

2.3 Real-World Analogy: Programming as Cooking

Understanding programming can be made easier with the analogy of cooking. Just as a recipe guides a chef, code guides a computer.

2.3.1 Ingredients as Variables

In cooking, ingredients are the raw materials used to create a dish. In programming, variables store the raw data used to create solutions.

Example:

- Ingredient: 1 cup of sugar → Variable: sugar = 1
- Programming analogy:

  python

sugar = 1

flour = 2

2.3.2 Steps in a Recipe as Instructions

A recipe provides step-by-step instructions for combining ingredients. Similarly, programming uses control structures to define the sequence of operations.

Example:

- Recipe: Mix sugar and flour, then bake.
- Python code:

python

```
batter = sugar + flour
print("Bake the batter")
```

2.3.3 Adjusting the Recipe as Debugging

If the dish doesn't taste right, the chef revises the recipe. In programming, if the output isn't as expected, the programmer debugs and fixes the code.

Example:

- Realizing you added too much sugar and fixing the measurement.
- Debugging in Python:

python

sugar = 0.5 # Adjust sugar quantity

2.4 Why Learn Programming?

Programming is more than a technical skill; it's a way of thinking. Here are a few reasons to learn it:

1. **Problem-Solving**:
   o Break down complex problems into smaller, manageable steps.
2. **Creativity**:
   o Build applications, games, or tools that solve real-world problems or bring your ideas to life.
3. **Career Opportunities**:
   o Programming opens doors to lucrative and impactful careers in tech, healthcare, finance, and more.

Programming is the art of instructing computers to solve problems, automate tasks, and create innovative solutions. From its roots in binary code to modern high-level languages like Python and Java, programming has evolved to become more accessible and versatile. By understanding code as instructions—similar to a recipe—you can start to see how programming applies to countless real-world scenarios.

In the next chapter, we'll compare Python and Java, exploring their unique strengths and real-world applications to help you understand why we'll focus on these two languages throughout the book. Let's dive in!

CHAPTER 3: PYTHON VS. JAVA: WHY THESE LANGUAGES?

When learning programming, the choice of language can feel overwhelming. Python and Java, two of the most popular programming languages, offer distinct advantages, making them ideal for a wide range of applications. This chapter explores why Python and Java are excellent languages for beginners and professionals, highlighting their strengths and real-world applications.

3.1 Why Python and Java?

Python and Java dominate the programming landscape for their combination of power, versatility, and accessibility. Together, these languages cover an extensive range of use cases, from automation and web development to large-scale enterprise solutions.

3.1.1 Python: Simplicity Meets Versatility

Python is often described as a "batteries-included" language because it provides a wide array of tools and libraries out of the box. It is beginner-friendly yet robust enough for complex applications.

3.2 Python: Simplicity and Versatility

Python is designed to prioritize readability and simplicity, making it an excellent choice for beginners and professionals alike.

3.2.1 Simplicity

- **Readable Syntax**: Python's syntax closely resembles natural language, reducing the learning curve.

  python

  print("Hello, World!")
  This simple command outputs a message to the screen. Compare this to other languages with more verbose syntax, and Python becomes an obvious choice for beginners.

- **Minimal Boilerplate Code**: Python avoids unnecessary syntax, allowing developers to focus on solving problems rather than managing code structure.

3.2.2 Versatility

Python excels in various domains, thanks to its extensive libraries and frameworks:

- **Data Science and Machine Learning**: Libraries like **pandas**, **NumPy**, and **scikit-learn** make Python the preferred language for data analysis and AI research.
- **Web Development**: Frameworks like **Django** and **Flask** power dynamic and scalable websites.
- **Automation**: Python scripts can automate repetitive tasks, such as file management or data entry.

3.2.3 Real-World Example: Python for Automation

Python's simplicity makes it ideal for automating tedious tasks. Here's a Python script to rename files in a folder:

python

```
import os

folder_path = "C:/example_folder"
for count, filename in enumerate(os.listdir(folder_path)):
    new_name = f"file_{count}.txt"
    os.rename(os.path.join(folder_path,                  filename),
os.path.join(folder_path, new_name))
```

This script renames all files in the folder to file_0.txt, file_1.txt, and so on—saving hours of manual work.

3.3 Java: Robustness and Platform Independence

While Python shines in simplicity, Java is a powerhouse for building robust, scalable, and portable applications. It's the backbone of many enterprise-grade systems and continues to be a staple in software development.

3.3.1 Robustness

- **Strong Typing**: Java enforces type safety, which helps catch errors at compile time, leading to fewer runtime issues.

  java

  int age = 25; // Ensures that "age" is always an integer

- **Rich Libraries and APIs**: Java provides extensive libraries for tasks such as networking, database management, and cryptography.

3.3.2 Platform Independence

Java's slogan, "Write Once, Run Anywhere," encapsulates its greatest strength. Programs written in Java can run on any platform with a Java Virtual Machine (JVM), eliminating compatibility concerns.

3.3.3 Real-World Example: Java for Enterprise Applications

Java's robustness makes it the language of choice for enterprise applications that demand reliability and scalability. Here's a simplified example of a Java program that connects to a database:

java

```
import java.sql.Connection;
import java.sql.DriverManager;
import java.sql.Statement;

public class DatabaseExample {
    public static void main(String[] args) {
        try {
            Connection connection = DriverManager.getConnection("jdbc:mysql://localhost:3306/mydb", "user", "password");
            Statement stmt = connection.createStatement();
            stmt.executeUpdate("INSERT INTO users (name, age) VALUES ('Alice', 30)");
            connection.close();
        } catch (Exception e) {
            e.printStackTrace();
        }
```

```
    }
}
```

This program connects to a MySQL database and inserts a new user record, showcasing Java's suitability for enterprise-level data handling.

3.4 Comparing Python and Java

Feature	Python	Java
Syntax	Simple, beginner-friendly	Verbose but strict and reliable
Typing	Dynamic typing	Strong, static typing
Speed	Slower due to interpretation	Faster due to compilation
Use Cases	Data science, automation, web development	Enterprise systems, Android apps, large-scale systems
Community	Extensive libraries for diverse applications	Strong support for enterprise and mobile apps
Learning	Easier for beginners	Slightly steeper for

Feature	Python	Java
Curve		newcomers

3.5 Real-World Scenarios: Choosing Between Python and Java

Understanding when to use Python or Java depends on the project's requirements. Let's explore a few scenarios:

3.5.1 Scenario 1: Automating Business Processes

A company needs to automate repetitive data entry tasks. Python is ideal due to its simplicity and rich libraries for automation.

Solution:

- Use Python's **pandas** to process data.
- Automate web interactions with libraries like **Selenium**.

3.5.2 Scenario 2: Building a Banking System

A bank requires a secure, scalable system to manage customer accounts. Java's robustness and strong typing make it the best choice.

Solution:

- Use Java to build a backend with robust error handling.
- Leverage Java's security APIs for encrypted transactions.

3.5.3 Scenario 3: Developing a Mobile App

An e-commerce startup wants to launch an Android app. Java is the preferred language for native Android development.

Solution:

- Build the app using Android Studio, which is optimized for Java.

3.6 Why Learn Both?

Learning both Python and Java gives you the flexibility to tackle diverse challenges:

- Start with Python for its simplicity and immediate feedback.
- Transition to Java to understand enterprise-level development and strong typing.

Together, these languages form a comprehensive foundation for your programming journey.

Python and Java each have unique strengths, making them valuable tools for any programmer. Python's simplicity and versatility shine in automation, data analysis, and web development, while Java's robustness and platform independence make it indispensable for enterprise applications and mobile development. By learning both, you'll gain a versatile skill set that prepares you for a wide range of projects.

In the next chapter, we'll set up your development environment for Python and Java, guiding you through the installation of tools and writing your first programs. Let's start coding!

CHAPTER 4: SETTING UP YOUR DEVELOPMENT ENVIRONMENT

Before diving into programming, it's essential to set up a development environment that allows you to write, test, and debug your code efficiently. This chapter will guide you through installing Python and Java, introduce you to Integrated Development Environments (IDEs), and help you write your first "Hello, World!" program in both languages.

4.1 Installing Python and Java

Python and Java are platform-independent, meaning they can run on various operating systems like Windows, macOS, and Linux. Let's walk through the installation process for both.

4.1.1 Installing Python

1. **Download Python**:
   - Visit the Python official website.
   - Download the latest stable version of Python for your operating system.
2. **Install Python**:

- o Run the installer.
- o Ensure the option **Add Python to PATH** is selected.
- o Click **Install Now** and follow the prompts.

3. **Verify Installation**:

- o Open your terminal or command prompt.
- o Type python --version or python3 --version.
- o You should see the installed Python version, e.g., Python 3.10.6.

4. **Install pip**:

- o pip is Python's package manager, usually installed by default.
- o Verify by typing pip --version. If not installed, run:

sh

python -m ensurepip

4.1.2 Installing Java

1. **Download Java**:

- o Visit the Oracle Java SE Downloads or use an open-source alternative like OpenJDK.

2. **Install Java**:

- o Run the installer and follow the instructions.

- o Ensure you note the installation directory (e.g., C:\Program Files\Java).

3. **Set Environment Variables** (Windows users):
   - o Add the Java bin directory to your system's PATH:
     - Open **System Properties** > **Environment Variables**.
     - Under **System Variables**, find **Path** and click **Edit**.
     - Add the path to the Java bin folder (e.g., C:\Program Files\Java\bin).

4. **Verify Installation**:
   - o Open your terminal or command prompt.
   - o Type java --version and javac --version.
   - o You should see the installed Java version, e.g., Java 17.0.2.

4.2 Introduction to IDEs

An Integrated Development Environment (IDE) provides tools like code editors, debuggers, and project management features in a single interface, making coding more efficient.

4.2.1 PyCharm

- **Why PyCharm?**
    - Tailored for Python development.
    - Features intelligent code completion, debugging, and built-in tools like version control.
- **Installation**:
    - Download from PyCharm official site.
    - Install the **Community Edition** (free) or **Professional Edition** (paid).
- **Setup**:
    - Open PyCharm and create a new project.
    - Choose a Python interpreter for the project.

4.2.2 IntelliJ IDEA

- **Why IntelliJ IDEA?**
    - Ideal for Java development with robust support for frameworks, debugging, and integration with build tools like Maven.
- **Installation**:
    - Download from IntelliJ IDEA official site.
    - Install the **Community Edition** (free) or **Ultimate Edition** (paid).
- **Setup**:
    - Open IntelliJ IDEA and create a new project.

- o Configure a Java SDK by selecting the Java installation directory.

4.2.3 Visual Studio Code

- **Why Visual Studio Code?**
  - o Lightweight and versatile, with support for multiple languages through extensions.
  - o Excellent for both Python and Java development.
- **Installation**:
  - o Download from Visual Studio Code official site.
- **Setup**:
  - o Install extensions for Python and Java:
    - **Python Extension** by Microsoft.
    - **Java Extension Pack** by Microsoft.
  - o Configure interpreters for Python and Java.

4.3 Writing Your First "Hello, World!" Program

Let's start coding! A "Hello, World!" program is a simple program that outputs the text "Hello, World!" to the screen.

4.3.1 "Hello, World!" in Python

1. **Write the Code**:
   - Open your IDE (e.g., PyCharm or Visual Studio Code).
   - Create a new Python file (e.g., hello.py).
   - Enter the following code:

   ```python
   print("Hello, World!")
   ```

2. **Run the Program**:
   - In PyCharm, click the **Run** button or press Shift + F10.
   - In Visual Studio Code, right-click the editor and select **Run Python File in Terminal**.
   - You should see the output: Hello, World!.

4.3.2 "Hello, World!" in Java

1. **Write the Code**:
   - Open your IDE (e.g., IntelliJ IDEA or Visual Studio Code).
   - Create a new Java file (e.g., HelloWorld.java).

- o Enter the following code:

java

```
public class HelloWorld {
    public static void main(String[] args) {
        System.out.println("Hello, World!");
    }
}
```

2. **Compile and Run the Program**:
   - o In IntelliJ IDEA, click the **Run** button or press Shift + F10.
   - o In Visual Studio Code, use the **Java Extension Pack** to run the program.
   - o You should see the output: Hello, World!.

4.4 Troubleshooting Installation Issues

1. **Python Path Issues**:
   - o If Python isn't recognized, ensure it's added to the PATH environment variable during installation.
   - o Check by typing where python in the terminal (Windows) or which python (macOS/Linux).
2. **Java Version Conflicts**:

o   If multiple Java versions are installed, configure the JAVA_HOME environment variable to point to the correct version.

3. **IDE Configuration Errors**:
   o   Ensure you've correctly linked interpreters or SDKs in your IDE settings.

Setting up your development environment is the first step toward programming proficiency. By installing Python and Java and using IDEs like PyCharm, IntelliJ IDEA, and Visual Studio Code, you've prepared the tools needed for efficient coding. Writing and running your first "Hello, World!" program is a milestone that marks the beginning of your journey into computer science.

In the next chapter, we'll explore programming fundamentals, including variables, data types, and how computers store and manipulate data. Let's continue building your coding skills!

CHAPTER 5: UNDERSTANDING VARIABLES AND DATA TYPES

Variables and data types are the building blocks of programming. A variable is like a container that holds information, and the data type defines the kind of information that can be stored. In this chapter, we'll explore how computers store data in memory, understand common data types, and work through a real-world example of calculating a shopping bill.

5.1 Variables and Memory: How Computers Store Data

5.1.1 What Are Variables?

A **variable** is a named space in a computer's memory that stores data. It allows us to:

- Temporarily hold values.
- Refer to those values using meaningful names.

Example: In Python:

python

price = 10.99 # A variable named 'price' holds the value 10.99
In Java:

java

double price = 10.99; // A variable named 'price' holds the value 10.99

5.1.2 How Do Computers Store Variables?

When you declare a variable:

1. **Memory Allocation**:
   - The computer assigns a block of memory to store the value.
   - The size of memory depends on the data type (e.g., integers use less memory than strings).
2. **Variable Name**:
   - Acts as a label to access the memory block.

5.1.3 Naming Variables

Variable names should:

- Start with a letter or an underscore (_).
- Be descriptive (e.g., total_price instead of x).

Example:

python

quantity = 5 # Good naming

x = 5   # Not descriptive

5.2 Data Types

Data types define the kind of data a variable can hold. Each programming language supports a variety of data types, but here we'll focus on the most common ones: integers, floats, strings, and booleans.

5.2.1 Integer (int)

An **integer** is a whole number without decimal points.

Example:

- Python:

  python

  age = 25

- Java:

  java

int age = 25;

Uses:

- Counting items.
- Representing IDs.

5.2.2 Float (or double in Java)

A **float** is a number that includes decimal points. In Java, a more precise version is called double.

Example:

- Python:

python

temperature = 36.5

- Java:

java

double temperature = 36.5;

Uses:

- Representing measurements like weight or height.
- Calculations involving fractions.

5.2.3 String

A **string** is a sequence of characters used to represent text.

Example:

- Python:

  python

  name = "Alice"

- Java:

  java

  String name = "Alice";

Uses:

- Storing names, messages, or descriptions.

5.2.4 Boolean

A **boolean** holds one of two values: True or False (in Python) or true or false (in Java).

Example:

- Python:

  python

  is_raining = False

- Java:

  java

  boolean isRaining = false;

Uses:

- Decision-making in programs.
- Representing conditions like "is the user logged in?"

5.3 Real-World Example: Calculating a Shopping Bill

Let's apply our understanding of variables and data types to solve a real-world problem: calculating the total bill for a shopping trip.

5.3.1 Problem Description

A user buys several items from a store. Each item has a name, quantity, and price. We need to calculate the total cost.

5.3.2 Solution in Python

1. Define variables for items:

python

```python
item1_name = "Apples"
item1_quantity = 3
item1_price = 1.5
```

2. Calculate the cost:

python

```python
total_cost = item1_quantity * item1_price
```

3. Print the bill:

python

```python
print(f"Item: {item1_name}, Quantity: {item1_quantity}, Price per unit: ${item1_price}")
print(f"Total Cost: ${total_cost}")
```

Output:

yaml

Item: Apples, Quantity: 3, Price per unit: $1.5

Total Cost: $4.5

5.3.3 Solution in Java

1. Define variables for items:

java

```java
public class ShoppingBill {
    public static void main(String[] args) {
        String item1Name = "Apples";
        int item1Quantity = 3;
        double item1Price = 1.5;
```

2. Calculate the cost:

java

```java
double totalCost = item1Quantity * item1Price;
```

3. Print the bill:

java

```
        System.out.println("Item:    "  +   item1Name  +   ",
Quantity: " + item1Quantity + ", Price per unit: $" +
item1Price);
        System.out.println("Total Cost: $" + totalCost);
    }
}
```

Output:

yaml

Item: Apples, Quantity: 3, Price per unit: $1.5
Total Cost: $4.5

5.4 Common Errors with Variables and Data Types

1. **Mismatched Data Types**:
    o   Example: Trying to multiply a string by a float.
    o   Python:

    python

    print("5" * 2.5) # Causes an error

    o   Java:

    java

System.out.println("5" * 2.5); // Causes an error

2. **Uninitialized Variables**:
  - Using variables before assigning values can cause errors.
  - Python:

python

print(total) # NameError: name 'total' is not defined

  - Java:

java

int total;
System.out.println(total);   // Compilation error: variable might not have been initialized

Variables and data types are essential to programming, enabling you to store and manipulate information effectively. Integers, floats, strings, and booleans allow you to represent numbers, text, and conditions in your programs. By understanding how to use them, you can begin solving practical problems like calculating a shopping bill.

In the next chapter, we'll explore control structures—if-else statements and loops—that allow programs to make decisions and repeat actions. Let's keep building!

CHAPTER 6: CONTROL STRUCTURES: IF-ELSE AND LOOPS

Control structures are essential for creating dynamic and flexible programs. They enable decision-making and repetition, allowing a program to react to conditions and perform tasks repeatedly. In this chapter, you'll learn how to:

- Make decisions with **if-else statements**.
- Use **for** and **while loops** to repeat tasks.
- Apply these concepts in a real-world example to calculate discounts.

6.1 Decision-Making with If-Else Statements

The **if-else** statement allows a program to make decisions based on conditions.

6.1.1 How If-Else Statements Work

- The **if** block is executed if the condition evaluates to True (Python) or true (Java).

- The **else** block is executed when the condition evaluates to False (Python) or false (Java).

Basic Syntax:

- Python:

python

```
if condition:
    # Code to execute if condition is true
else:
    # Code to execute if condition is false
```

- Java:

java

```
if (condition) {
    // Code to execute if condition is true
} else {
    // Code to execute if condition is false
}
```

6.1.2 Example: Check for Discounts

Let's write a Python and Java program to check if a customer qualifies for a discount.

- **Python**:

python

```
total_purchase = 150

if total_purchase > 100:
    print("You qualify for a discount!")
else:
    print("No discount available.")
```

- **Java**:

java

```
int totalPurchase = 150;

if (totalPurchase > 100) {
    System.out.println("You qualify for a discount!");
} else {
    System.out.println("No discount available.");
}
```

Output:

css

You qualify for a discount!

6.1.3 Adding Multiple Conditions

For more complex decisions, use elif in Python or else if in Java.

- **Python**:

python

```
if total_purchase > 200:
    print("You get a 20% discount!")
elif total_purchase > 100:
    print("You get a 10% discount!")
else:
    print("No discount available.")
```

- **Java**:

java

```
if (totalPurchase > 200) {
    System.out.println("You get a 20% discount!");
} else if (totalPurchase > 100) {
    System.out.println("You get a 10% discount!");
```

```
} else {
    System.out.println("No discount available.");
}
```

6.2 Iterating with For and While Loops

Loops allow you to execute a block of code multiple times. Unity's two primary loop types are **for** and **while** loops.

6.2.1 The For Loop

The **for** loop iterates over a sequence (Python) or runs a specific number of times (Java).

Syntax:

- Python:

  python

  ```
  for variable in sequence:
      # Code to execute in each iteration
  ```

- Java:

  java

```
for (initialization; condition; update) {
    // Code to execute in each iteration
}
```

Example:

- Print numbers 1 to 5.
- **Python**:

python

```
for i in range(1, 6):
    print(i)
```

- **Java**:

java

```
for (int i = 1; i <= 5; i++) {
    System.out.println(i);
}
```

Output:

```
1
2
3
4
```

5

6.2.2 The While Loop

The **while** loop repeats as long as a condition is true.

Syntax:

- Python:

  python

  ```
  while condition:
      # Code to execute
  ```

- Java:

  java

  ```
  while (condition) {
      // Code to execute
  }
  ```

Example:

- Countdown from 5 to 1.
- **Python**:

  python

```
countdown = 5
while countdown > 0:
    print(countdown)
    countdown -= 1
```

- **Java**:

java

```
int countdown = 5;
while (countdown > 0) {
    System.out.println(countdown);
    countdown--;
}
```

Output:

```
5
4
3
2
1
```

6.2.3 Infinite Loops

If the condition in a loop is always true, the loop runs indefinitely. These should be avoided unless explicitly required.

Example (Python):

python

```
while True:
    print("This is an infinite loop.")
```

6.3 Real-World Example: Calculating Discounts

Let's combine **if-else** statements and loops to write a program that calculates the total discount for multiple items in a customer's shopping cart.

6.3.1 Problem Description

A store offers a 10% discount on items costing more than $50. Calculate the total discount for all eligible items in the shopping cart.

6.3.2 Solution in Python

1. Define a list of item prices.

2. Use a loop to iterate through each item.

3. Check if the item qualifies for a discount using an if-else statement.

4. Calculate the total discount.

Python Code:

python

```
cart = [30, 70, 120, 45]
total_discount = 0

for price in cart:
    if price > 50:
        discount = price * 0.10
        total_discount += discount

print(f"Total Discount: ${total_discount:.2f}")
```

Output:

bash

Total Discount: $19.00

6.3.3 Solution in Java

1. Define an array of item prices.

2. Use a for loop to iterate through each item.

3. Apply an if-else statement to calculate discounts.

4. Print the total discount.

Java Code:

java

```java
public class DiscountCalculator {
    public static void main(String[] args) {
        double[] cart = {30, 70, 120, 45};
        double totalDiscount = 0;

        for (double price : cart) {
            if (price > 50) {
                double discount = price * 0.10;
                totalDiscount += discount;
            }
        }

        System.out.printf("Total Discount: $%.2f%n", totalDiscount);
    }
}
```
Output:

bash

Total Discount: $19.00

6.4 Common Errors with If-Else and Loops

1. **Off-By-One Errors**:
   o   Starting or ending a loop at the wrong index.
   o   Example: Using range(0, 5) instead of range(1, 6).
2. **Infinite Loops**:
   o   Forgetting to update the condition in a while loop.
3. **Misplaced Conditions**:
   o   Placing an else block incorrectly, leading to unexpected behavior.

Control structures enable dynamic and repetitive programming. **If-else statements** allow decision-making based on conditions, while **loops** (for and while) handle repetitive tasks. Combining these tools, we created a program to calculate discounts for a shopping cart. Understanding these structures is essential for building more complex and interactive programs.

In the next chapter, we'll delve into **functions and methods**, learning how to write reusable and modular code. Let's continue coding!

CHAPTER 7: FUNCTIONS AND METHODS

Functions and methods are fundamental in programming, enabling you to write reusable, modular, and organized code. This chapter introduces you to defining and calling functions in Python and Java, explains how to pass arguments and return values, and walks through a real-world example: building a simple calculator application.

7.1 What Are Functions and Methods?

A **function** is a reusable block of code that performs a specific task. In Python, functions are standalone, while in Java, functions are typically referred to as **methods** and are associated with classes.

Why Use Functions?

- **Reusability**: Write once, use multiple times.
- **Modularity**: Break complex tasks into smaller, manageable parts.
- **Readability**: Code is easier to read and maintain.

7.2 Defining and Calling Functions

7.2.1 Syntax for Defining Functions

- **Python**:
  - o   Use the def keyword to define a function.

python

```
def function_name(parameters):
   # Code block
   return value
```

- **Java**:
  - o   Define methods inside a class using a return type and parameters.

java

```
public returnType methodName(parameters) {
   // Code block
   return value;
}
```

7.2.2 Example: Printing a Message

- **Python**:

python

```
def greet():
    print("Hello, World!")

greet()  # Calling the function
```

- **Java**:

java

```
public class Main {
    public static void greet() {
        System.out.println("Hello, World!");
    }

    public static void main(String[] args) {
        greet();  // Calling the method
    }
}
```

Output:

Hello, World!

7.3 Passing Arguments and Returning Values

7.3.1 Passing Arguments

- Arguments are inputs you provide to functions.
- **Python**:

python

```python
def greet(name):
    print(f"Hello, {name}!")


greet("Alice")
```

- **Java**:

java

```java
public static void greet(String name) {
    System.out.println("Hello, " + name + "!");
}

public static void main(String[] args) {
    greet("Alice");
}
```
Output:

Hello, Alice!

7.3.2 Returning Values

- Functions can return values to the caller.
- **Python**:

python

```python
def add(a, b):
    return a + b

result = add(5, 3)
print(result)
```

- **Java**:

java

```java
public static int add(int a, int b) {
    return a + b;
}

public static void main(String[] args) {
    int result = add(5, 3);
    System.out.println(result);
}
```

Output:

8

7.3.3 Default and Optional Parameters

- Functions can have default values for parameters.
- **Python**:

python

```
def greet(name="Guest"):
    print(f"Hello, {name}!")

greet()  # Uses default value
greet("Alice")
```

- **Java** does not support default arguments directly, but you can achieve similar behavior using method overloading.
- **Java**:

java

```
public static void greet() {
    System.out.println("Hello, Guest!");
}
```

```java
public static void greet(String name) {
    System.out.println("Hello, " + name + "!");
}

public static void main(String[] args) {
    greet();  // Calls the no-argument method
    greet("Alice");
}
```

Output:

Hello, Guest!

Hello, Alice!

7.4 Real-World Example: Building a Calculator Application

Let's build a simple calculator that performs basic arithmetic operations: addition, subtraction, multiplication, and division.

7.4.1 Python Calculator

1. Define a function for each operation.
2. Use input prompts to get user data.
3. Call the appropriate function based on user choice.

Python Code:

python

```python
def add(a, b):
    return a + b

def subtract(a, b):
    return a - b

def multiply(a, b):
    return a * b

def divide(a, b):
    if b != 0:
        return a / b
    else:
        return "Error: Division by zero"

print("Select operation:")
print("1. Add")
print("2. Subtract")
print("3. Multiply")
print("4. Divide")

choice = input("Enter choice (1/2/3/4): ")
```

```python
num1 = float(input("Enter first number: "))
num2 = float(input("Enter second number: "))


if choice == '1':
    print("Result:", add(num1, num2))
elif choice == '2':
    print("Result:", subtract(num1, num2))
elif choice == '3':
    print("Result:", multiply(num1, num2))
elif choice == '4':
    print("Result:", divide(num1, num2))
else:
    print("Invalid input")
```

7.4.2 Java Calculator

1. Define methods for each operation.
2. Use a Scanner object to get user input.
3. Call the appropriate method based on user choice.

Java Code:

java


```java
import java.util.Scanner;
```

```java
public class Calculator {

    public static double add(double a, double b) {
        return a + b;
    }

    public static double subtract(double a, double b) {
        return a - b;
    }

    public static double multiply(double a, double b) {
        return a * b;
    }

    public static double divide(double a, double b) {
        if (b != 0) {
            return a / b;
        } else {
            System.out.println("Error: Division by zero");
            return 0;
        }
    }

    public static void main(String[] args) {
        Scanner scanner = new Scanner(System.in);
```

```java
System.out.println("Select operation:");
System.out.println("1. Add");
System.out.println("2. Subtract");
System.out.println("3. Multiply");
System.out.println("4. Divide");

int choice = scanner.nextInt();

System.out.print("Enter first number: ");
double num1 = scanner.nextDouble();

System.out.print("Enter second number: ");
double num2 = scanner.nextDouble();

switch (choice) {
    case 1:
        System.out.println("Result: " + add(num1, num2));
        break;
    case 2:
        System.out.println("Result: " + subtract(num1, num2));
        break;
    case 3:
        System.out.println("Result: " + multiply(num1, num2));
        break;
```

```
        case 4:
            System.out.println("Result: " + divide(num1, num2));
            break;
        default:
            System.out.println("Invalid choice");
    }

        scanner.close();
    }
}
```

Sample Output (Python or Java):

mathematica

Select operation:
1. Add
2. Subtract
3. Multiply
4. Divide
Enter choice (1/2/3/4): 1
Enter first number: 10
Enter second number: 5
Result: 15.0

7.5 Best Practices for Functions

1. **Keep Functions Focused**:
   - Each function should perform a single task.
   - Avoid mixing unrelated logic in one function.

2. **Use Descriptive Names**:
   - Function names should clearly indicate their purpose (e.g., calculate_total).

3. **Document Your Functions**:
   - Add comments or docstrings to explain what the function does.

Python Example:

python

```
def calculate_total(price, quantity):
    """
    Calculate the total cost of an item.
    :param price: The price of the item
    :param quantity: The quantity purchased
    :return: Total cost
    """
    return price * quantity
```

Functions and methods are essential tools for creating reusable and organized code. You've learned how to define, call, and pass arguments to functions in Python and Java, and explored how to return values. By building a calculator application, you applied these concepts to a practical problem, demonstrating how functions simplify complex tasks.

In the next chapter, we'll dive into **working with strings**, exploring methods for manipulating and formatting text in Python and Java. Let's keep coding!

CHAPTER 8: WORKING WITH STRINGS

Strings are one of the most widely used data types in programming. They represent sequences of characters and are essential for storing and manipulating text. This chapter explores:

- Techniques for string manipulation and formatting.
- A comparison of string libraries and methods in Python and Java.
- A real-world example: Building a simple text analyzer.

8.1 String Manipulation and Formatting

String manipulation involves changing, analyzing, or transforming strings, while string formatting helps structure text for display or output.

8.1.1 String Basics

A string is a sequence of characters enclosed in quotes. In Python, you use single (') or double quotes ("), while in Java, strings are enclosed in double quotes.

- **Python:**

python

greeting = "Hello, World!"

- **Java**:

java

String greeting = "Hello, World!";

8.1.2 Common String Operations

1. Concatenation Joining two or more strings.

- **Python**:

python

```
first_name = "John"
last_name = "Doe"
full_name = first_name + " " + last_name
print(full_name)  # Output: John Doe
```

- **Java**:

java

String firstName = "John";

```
String lastName = "Doe";
String fullName = firstName + " " + lastName;
System.out.println(fullName);  // Output: John Doe
```

2. Slicing/Substrings Extracting part of a string.

- **Python**:

python

```
text = "Hello, World!"
print(text[0:5])  # Output: Hello
```

- **Java**:

java

```
String text = "Hello, World!";
System.out.println(text.substring(0, 5));  // Output: Hello
```

3. String Length Finding the number of characters in a string.

- **Python**:

python

```
print(len("Hello"))  # Output: 5
```

- **Java**:

java

```
System.out.println("Hello".length());  // Output: 5
```

8.1.3 String Formatting

Formatting strings allows you to embed variables and structure text for readability.

Python:

- Using f-strings:

python

```
name = "Alice"
age = 30
print(f"My name is {name}, and I am {age} years old.")
```

Java:

- Using String.format:

java

```
String name = "Alice";
int age = 30;
System.out.println(String.format("My name is %s, and I
am %d years old.", name, age));
```

Output:

csharp

My name is Alice, and I am 30 years old.

8.2 Python vs. Java: String Libraries and Methods

Python and Java provide powerful libraries and methods for working with strings. Let's compare some commonly used features.

8.2.1 String Immutability

In both Python and Java, strings are immutable. Modifications create new string objects instead of altering the original.

Example:

- **Python**:

  python

  ```python
  text = "Hello"
  text = text + ", World!"
  print(text)  # Output: Hello, World!
  ```

- **Java**:

java

```
String text = "Hello";
text = text + ", World!";
System.out.println(text);  // Output: Hello, World!
```

8.2.2 Common String Methods

Operation	Python	Java
Convert to lowercase	"Hello".lower()	"Hello".toLowerCase()
Convert to uppercase	"hello".upper()	"hello".toUpperCase()
Check if starts with	"Hello".startswith("H")	"Hello".startsWith("H")
Replace substring	"Hello".replace("H", "J")	"Hello".replace("H", "J")
Trim whitespace	" Hello ".strip()	" Hello ".trim()
Split into list/array	"a,b,c".split(",")	"a,b,c".split(",")
Join list/array	",".join(["a", "b", "c"])	String.join(",", "a", "b")

8.2.3 Regular Expressions

Regular expressions (regex) are powerful tools for pattern matching and manipulation. Python and Java have built-in support for regex.

- **Python** (via re module):

python

```
import re
pattern = r"\d+"  # Matches numbers
result = re.findall(pattern, "Order 123 contains 4 items")
print(result)  # Output: ['123', '4']
```

- **Java** (via Pattern and Matcher):

java

```
import java.util.regex.*;
Pattern pattern = Pattern.compile("\\d+");   // Matches numbers
Matcher matcher = pattern.matcher("Order 123 contains 4 items");
while (matcher.find()) {
    System.out.println(matcher.group()); // Output: 123, 4
```

}

8.3 Real-World Example: Building a Simple Text Analyzer

Let's create a text analyzer that:

1. Counts the number of words.
2. Counts the number of sentences.
3. Identifies the most common word.

8.3.1 Python Solution

python

```python
from collections import Counter
import string

def analyze_text(text):
    # Remove punctuation and convert to lowercase
    cleaned_text = text.translate(str.maketrans("", "", string.punctuation)).lower()

    # Split text into words and sentences
    words = cleaned_text.split()
    sentences = text.split(".")
```

```
# Count words and find the most common word
word_count = len(words)
sentence_count = len(sentences) - 1   # Exclude the last empty
split
most_common_word = Counter(words).most_common(1)[0]

print(f"Total Words: {word_count}")
print(f"Total Sentences: {sentence_count}")
print(f"Most    Common    Word:    {most_common_word[0]}
({most_common_word[1]} times)")

# Sample text
sample = "Hello world! This is a test. Hello again."
analyze_text(sample)
```

Output:

mathematica

Total Words: 8
Total Sentences: 2
Most Common Word: hello (2 times)

8.3.2 Java Solution

java

```java
import java.util.*;
import java.util.regex.*;

public class TextAnalyzer {

    public static void analyzeText(String text) {
        // Remove punctuation and convert to lowercase
        String cleanedText = text.replaceAll("[^a-zA-Z ]",
"").toLowerCase();

        // Split text into words and sentences
        String[] words = cleanedText.split("\\s+");
        String[] sentences = text.split("\\.");

        // Count words and find the most common word
        int wordCount = words.length;
        int sentenceCount = sentences.length - 1;  // Exclude the last
empty split
        Map<String, Integer> wordFrequency = new HashMap<>();

        for (String word : words) {
            wordFrequency.put(word,
wordFrequency.getOrDefault(word, 0) + 1);
        }
```

```
    String              mostCommonWord              =
Collections.max(wordFrequency.entrySet(),
Map.Entry.comparingByValue()).getKey();


    System.out.println("Total Words: " + wordCount);
    System.out.println("Total Sentences: " + sentenceCount);
    System.out.println("Most    Common    Word:    "    +
mostCommonWord         +         "         ("         +
wordFrequency.get(mostCommonWord) + " times)");
  }


  public static void main(String[] args) {
    String sample = "Hello world! This is a test. Hello again.";
    analyzeText(sample);
  }
}
```

Output:

mathematica

Total Words: 8

Total Sentences: 2

Most Common Word: hello (2 times)

8.4 Best Practices for String Handling

1. **Minimize String Concatenation in Loops**:
   o Use StringBuilder in Java for efficiency.
2. **Sanitize Input**:
   o Remove unnecessary whitespace, punctuation, or malicious patterns.
3. **Use Built-In Methods**:
   o Take advantage of Python and Java's powerful string libraries.

Working with strings is a fundamental aspect of programming. In this chapter, you learned about string manipulation, formatting, and how Python and Java provide robust tools for handling text. By building a text analyzer, you applied these concepts to a practical example. Strings are essential for tasks ranging from user input processing to natural language analysis.

In the next chapter, we'll explore **lists, arrays, and dictionaries**, diving deeper into storing and organizing data in Python and Java. Let's continue coding!

CHAPTER 9: LISTS, ARRAYS, AND DICTIONARIES

Data structures are essential for storing and organizing data efficiently. This chapter covers:

- Storing data with **lists** in Python and **arrays** in Java.
- Using **dictionaries** in Python and **HashMaps** in Java for key-value pairs.
- A real-world example: Storing and retrieving customer data.

9.1 Storing Data with Lists and Arrays

Lists (in Python) and arrays (in Java) are used to store collections of items such as numbers, strings, or objects.

9.1.1 Lists in Python

A **list** is a flexible, dynamic data structure that can hold items of different types.

Key Features:

- Ordered.
- Allows duplicates.

- Can grow or shrink dynamically.

Example:

python

```
# Creating a list
fruits = ["apple", "banana", "cherry"]

# Accessing elements
print(fruits[0])  # Output: apple

# Adding elements
fruits.append("date")

# Removing elements
fruits.remove("banana")

# Iterating over a list
for fruit in fruits:
    print(fruit)
```

9.1.2 Arrays in Java

An **array** is a fixed-size collection of elements of the same type.

Key Features:

- Ordered.

- Fixed size.

- Homogeneous (all elements must be of the same type).

Example:

java

```
// Creating an array
String[] fruits = {"apple", "banana", "cherry"};

// Accessing elements
System.out.println(fruits[0]);  // Output: apple

// Modifying elements
fruits[1] = "blueberry";

// Iterating over an array
for (String fruit : fruits) {
    System.out.println(fruit);
}
```

Comparison: Lists vs. Arrays

Feature	Python Lists	Java Arrays

Feature	Python Lists	Java Arrays
Size	Dynamic (can grow/shrink)	Fixed (size defined at creation)
Data Type	Can hold mixed data types	All elements must be of the same type
Ease of Use	Built-in methods for manipulation	Requires manual handling of resizing

9.2 Dictionaries and HashMaps: Key-Value Pairs

Dictionaries (in Python) and HashMaps (in Java) are used to store data as key-value pairs. They allow quick lookups, updates, and deletions.

9.2.1 Dictionaries in Python

A **dictionary** is an unordered, mutable data structure where keys map to values.

Key Features:

- Keys must be unique and immutable (e.g., strings, numbers).
- Values can be of any type.

Example:

python

```
# Creating a dictionary
customer = {"id": 101, "name": "Alice", "age": 30}

# Accessing values
print(customer["name"])  # Output: Alice

# Adding or updating values
customer["email"] = "alice@example.com"

# Removing keys
del customer["age"]

# Iterating over keys and values
for key, value in customer.items():
    print(key, value)
```

9.2.2 HashMaps in Java

A **HashMap** is part of Java's java.util package and provides a similar key-value mapping.

Key Features:

- Keys must be unique.
- Allows null keys and values.
- Not synchronized (not thread-safe).

Example:

java

```
import java.util.HashMap;

public class Main {
    public static void main(String[] args) {
        // Creating a HashMap
        HashMap<String, String> customer = new HashMap<>();

        // Adding key-value pairs
        customer.put("id", "101");
        customer.put("name", "Alice");
        customer.put("age", "30");

        // Accessing values
        System.out.println(customer.get("name"));  // Output: Alice

        // Removing keys
        customer.remove("age");
```

```
// Iterating over keys and values
for (String key : customer.keySet()) {
   System.out.println(key + ": " + customer.get(key));
}
}
}
```

Comparison: Dictionaries vs. HashMaps

Feature	Python Dictionaries	Java HashMaps
Order	Ordered (from Python 3.7+)	Unordered
Null Support	No None keys, values allowed	Allows null keys and values
Thread Safety	Not thread-safe	Not thread-safe

9.3 Real-World Example: Storing and Retrieving Customer Data

9.3.1 Problem Description

A business needs to store customer information (ID, name, and email) and retrieve it efficiently using customer IDs.

9.3.2 Solution in Python

Use a dictionary to store customer data with customer IDs as keys.

Python Code:

python

```python
# Creating a dictionary of customers
customers = {
    101: {"name": "Alice", "email": "alice@example.com"},
    102: {"name": "Bob", "email": "bob@example.com"}
}

# Adding a new customer
customers[103] = {"name": "Charlie", "email": "charlie@example.com"}

# Retrieving customer information
customer_id = 102
if customer_id in customers:
    print(f"Customer {customer_id}: {customers[customer_id]['name']}, {customers[customer_id]['email']}")
else:
    print(f"Customer {customer_id} not found.")
```

```
# Removing a customer
del customers[101]
```

```
# Printing all customers
for id, details in customers.items():
    print(f"ID: {id}, Name: {details['name']}, Email: {details['email']}")
```

Output:

yaml

Customer 102: Bob, bob@example.com

ID: 102, Name: Bob, Email: bob@example.com

ID: 103, Name: Charlie, Email: charlie@example.com

9.3.3 Solution in Java

Use a HashMap to store customer data.

Java Code:

java

```java
import java.util.HashMap;

public class Main {
```

```
public static void main(String[] args) {
    // Creating a HashMap of customers
    HashMap<Integer, HashMap<String, String>> customers =
new HashMap<>();

    // Adding customers
    HashMap<String, String> customer1 = new HashMap<>();
    customer1.put("name", "Alice");
    customer1.put("email", "alice@example.com");
    customers.put(101, customer1);

    HashMap<String, String> customer2 = new HashMap<>();
    customer2.put("name", "Bob");
    customer2.put("email", "bob@example.com");
    customers.put(102, customer2);

    // Adding a new customer
    HashMap<String, String> customer3 = new HashMap<>();
    customer3.put("name", "Charlie");
    customer3.put("email", "charlie@example.com");
    customers.put(103, customer3);

    // Retrieving customer information
    int customerId = 102;
    if (customers.containsKey(customerId)) {
```

```
        HashMap<String,        String>        customer        =
customers.get(customerId);
        System.out.println("Customer  "  +  customerId  +  ":  "  +
customer.get("name") + ", " + customer.get("email"));
    } else {
        System.out.println("Customer  "  +  customerId  +  "  not
found.");
    }


    // Removing a customer
    customers.remove(101);


    // Printing all customers
    for (Integer id : customers.keySet()) {
        HashMap<String, String> details = customers.get(id);
        System.out.println("ID:   "   +   id   +   ",   Name:   "   +
details.get("name") + ", Email: " + details.get("email"));
    }
  }
}
```

Output:

yaml

Customer 102: Bob, bob@example.com

ID: 102, Name: Bob, Email: bob@example.com

ID: 103, Name: Charlie, Email: charlie@example.com

9.4 Best Practices for Lists, Arrays, and Dictionaries

1. **Choose the Right Data Structure**:
   o Use lists for ordered collections.
   o Use dictionaries or HashMaps for key-value pairs.
2. **Avoid Hardcoding**:
   o Populate data structures dynamically or load from external sources like files or databases.
3. **Iterate Efficiently**:
   o Use optimized loops or built-in methods for iteration.
4. **Handle Missing Keys Gracefully**:
   o Use methods like get (Python and Java) with default values to avoid errors.

In this chapter, you explored lists in Python and arrays in Java for storing ordered collections, as well as dictionaries and HashMaps for key-value mappings. Through a practical example of storing and retrieving customer data, you saw how these data structures make programming tasks efficient and intuitive. Mastery of these structures is essential for solving real-world problems in software development.

In the next chapter, we'll dive into **sorting and searching algorithms**, essential techniques for organizing and retrieving data effectively. Let's continue coding!

CHAPTER 10: SORTING AND SEARCHING ALGORITHMS

Sorting and searching algorithms are fundamental to efficient data organization and retrieval. This chapter covers:

- Introduction to sorting algorithms: **bubble sort** and **quicksort**.
- Understanding **binary search** for efficient lookups.
- Basics of time complexity analysis with Big-O notation.
- A real-world example: Sorting user scores in a game leaderboard.

10.1 Sorting Algorithms

Sorting algorithms rearrange elements in a dataset into a specific order, such as ascending or descending.

10.1.1 Bubble Sort

Bubble sort is a simple algorithm that repeatedly compares adjacent elements and swaps them if they are in the wrong order.

Steps:

1. Compare adjacent elements.

2. Swap them if the first is greater than the second.

3. Repeat until the list is sorted.

Python Implementation:

python

```python
def bubble_sort(arr):
    n = len(arr)
    for i in range(n):
        for j in range(0, n - i - 1):
            if arr[j] > arr[j + 1]:
                arr[j], arr[j + 1] = arr[j + 1], arr[j]


scores = [64, 34, 25, 12, 22, 11, 90]
bubble_sort(scores)
print(scores)  # Output: [11, 12, 22, 25, 34, 64, 90]
```

Java Implementation:

java

```java
public class BubbleSort {
    public static void bubbleSort(int[] arr) {
        int n = arr.length;
        for (int i = 0; i < n; i++) {
            for (int j = 0; j < n - i - 1; j++) {
```

```
        if (arr[j] > arr[j + 1]) {
            int temp = arr[j];
            arr[j] = arr[j + 1];
            arr[j + 1] = temp;
        }
      }
    }
  }

  public static void main(String[] args) {
    int[] scores = {64, 34, 25, 12, 22, 11, 90};
    bubbleSort(scores);
    for (int score : scores) {
      System.out.print(score + " ");
    }
  }
}
```

10.1.2 Quicksort

Quicksort is a divide-and-conquer algorithm that selects a "pivot" and partitions the array around the pivot, recursively sorting the subarrays.

Steps:

1. Choose a pivot.

2. Partition the array into elements less than and greater than the pivot.

3. Recursively apply the process to the subarrays.

Python Implementation:

python

```
def quicksort(arr):
    if len(arr) <= 1:
        return arr
    pivot = arr[len(arr) // 2]
    left = [x for x in arr if x < pivot]
    middle = [x for x in arr if x == pivot]
    right = [x for x in arr if x > pivot]
    return quicksort(left) + middle + quicksort(right)


scores = [64, 34, 25, 12, 22, 11, 90]
sorted_scores = quicksort(scores)
print(sorted_scores)  # Output: [11, 12, 22, 25, 34, 64, 90]
```

Java Implementation:

java

```
import java.util.Arrays;


public class QuickSort {
```

```
public static void quickSort(int[] arr, int low, int high) {
    if (low < high) {
        int pi = partition(arr, low, high);
        quickSort(arr, low, pi - 1);
        quickSort(arr, pi + 1, high);
    }
}


public static int partition(int[] arr, int low, int high) {
    int pivot = arr[high];
    int i = (low - 1);
    for (int j = low; j < high; j++) {
        if (arr[j] < pivot) {
            i++;
            int temp = arr[i];
            arr[i] = arr[j];
            arr[j] = temp;
        }
    }
    int temp = arr[i + 1];
    arr[i + 1] = arr[high];
    arr[high] = temp;
    return i + 1;
}
```

```
public static void main(String[] args) {
    int[] scores = {64, 34, 25, 12, 22, 11, 90};
    quickSort(scores, 0, scores.length - 1);
    System.out.println(Arrays.toString(scores));   // Output: [11, 12, 22, 25, 34, 64, 90]
    }
}
```

10.2 Searching Algorithms

Searching algorithms locate an element within a dataset.

10.2.1 Binary Search

Binary search is an efficient algorithm that works on sorted datasets by repeatedly dividing the search interval in half.

Steps:

1. Start with the middle element.
2. If the target is less than the middle, search the left half.
3. If the target is greater, search the right half.
4. Repeat until the element is found or the search interval is empty.

Python Implementation:

python

```python
def binary_search(arr, target):
    left, right = 0, len(arr) - 1
    while left <= right:
        mid = (left + right) // 2
        if arr[mid] == target:
            return mid
        elif arr[mid] < target:
            left = mid + 1
        else:
            right = mid - 1
    return -1


scores = [11, 12, 22, 25, 34, 64, 90]
index = binary_search(scores, 25)
print(index)  # Output: 3
```

Java Implementation:

java

```java
public class BinarySearch {
    public static int binarySearch(int[] arr, int target) {
        int left = 0, right = arr.length - 1;
        while (left <= right) {
            int mid = (left + right) / 2;
```

```
      if (arr[mid] == target) {
         return mid;
      } else if (arr[mid] < target) {
         left = mid + 1;
      } else {
         right = mid - 1;
      }
   }
   return -1;
}


public static void main(String[] args) {
   int[] scores = {11, 12, 22, 25, 34, 64, 90};
   int index = binarySearch(scores, 25);
   System.out.println(index);  // Output: 3
}
}
```

10.3 Analyzing Time Complexity: Big-O Basics

Big-O notation describes the efficiency of an algorithm in terms of time or space as input size grows.

Common Big-O Notations:

1. **O(1)**: Constant time, unaffected by input size.

2. **O(log n)**: Logarithmic time, e.g., binary search.

3. **O(n)**: Linear time, e.g., traversing a list.

4. **O(n^2)**: Quadratic time, e.g., bubble sort.

Algorithm	Best Case	Worst Case	Big-O
Bubble Sort	O(n)	O(n^2)	Inefficient
Quicksort	O(n log n)	O(n^2)	Efficient
Binary Search	O(1)	O(log n)	Very efficient

10.4 Real-World Example: Sorting User Scores in a Game Leaderboard

Problem Description

A game stores user scores. You need to sort the scores in descending order and allow efficient lookups to find a specific user's rank.

Python Solution

python

```
def sort_scores(scores):
```

```python
    return sorted(scores, reverse=True)

def find_rank(scores, target):
    sorted_scores = sort_scores(scores)
    rank = sorted_scores.index(target) + 1
    return rank

scores = [64, 34, 25, 12, 22, 11, 90]
sorted_scores = sort_scores(scores)
print("Sorted Scores:", sorted_scores)  # Output: [90, 64, 34, 25, 22, 12, 11]
print("Rank of 25:", find_rank(scores, 25))  # Output: Rank of 25: 4
```

Java Solution
java

```java
import java.util.Arrays;
import java.util.Collections;

public class Leaderboard {
    public static Integer[] sortScores(Integer[] scores) {
        Arrays.sort(scores, Collections.reverseOrder());
        return scores;
    }
```

```java
public static int findRank(Integer[] scores, int target) {
    Integer[] sortedScores = sortScores(scores);
    for (int i = 0; i < sortedScores.length; i++) {
        if (sortedScores[i] == target) {
            return i + 1;
        }
    }
    return -1;
}


public static void main(String[] args) {
    Integer[] scores = {64, 34, 25, 12, 22, 11, 90};
    Integer[] sortedScores = sortScores(scores);
    System.out.println("Sorted          Scores:       "       +
Arrays.toString(sortedScores));  // Output: [90, 64, 34, 25, 22, 12,
11]
    System.out.println("Rank of 25: " + findRank(scores, 25));  //
Output: Rank of 25: 4
    }
}
```

Sorting and searching algorithms are crucial for efficient data processing. You learned about **bubble sort**, **quicksort**, and **binary search**, explored their time complexity, and applied them to sort and rank user scores in a game leaderboard. Understanding these algorithms equips you to handle various real-world scenarios where data organization and retrieval are essential.

In the next chapter, we'll explore **object-oriented programming (OOP)**, a paradigm that emphasizes reusability and modularity. Let's continue coding!

CHAPTER 11: OBJECT-ORIENTED PROGRAMMING (OOP)

Object-Oriented Programming (OOP) is a paradigm that models data and behavior as objects, enabling code that is modular, reusable, and easy to maintain. In this chapter, we'll explore:

- **Classes and objects** as the foundation of OOP.
- Key OOP principles: **inheritance**, **polymorphism**, and **encapsulation**.
- A real-world example: Designing a library management system.

11.1 Classes and Objects: Building Reusable Code

11.1.1 What Are Classes and Objects?

- **Class**: A blueprint for creating objects. It defines properties (attributes) and behaviors (methods).
- **Object**: An instance of a class with specific data and functionality.

Analogy:

- A class is like a blueprint for a car. The blueprint defines the attributes (e.g., color, model) and actions (e.g., start, stop). An object is the car built from the blueprint.

11.1.2 Defining Classes

- **Python**:

python

```
class Car:
    def __init__(self, brand, model):
        self.brand = brand
        self.model = model

    def start(self):
        print(f"{self.brand} {self.model} is starting.")

# Creating an object
car1 = Car("Toyota", "Corolla")
car1.start()  # Output: Toyota Corolla is starting.
```

- **Java**:

java

```java
public class Car {
    String brand;
    String model;

    public Car(String brand, String model) {
        this.brand = brand;
        this.model = model;
    }

    public void start() {
        System.out.println(brand + " " + model + " is starting.");
    }

    public static void main(String[] args) {
        Car car1 = new Car("Toyota", "Corolla");
        car1.start();  // Output: Toyota Corolla is starting.
    }
}
```

11.1.3 Objects and Attributes

Objects hold specific data defined by the class attributes.

- **Python**:

python

print(car1.brand) # Output: Toyota

- **Java**:

java

System.out.println(car1.brand); // Output: Toyota

11.2 OOP Principles

11.2.1 Inheritance

Inheritance allows a class (child) to derive properties and behaviors from another class (parent), enabling code reuse.

- **Python**:

python

```python
class Vehicle:
    def move(self):
        print("Vehicle is moving.")

class Car(Vehicle):
    def honk(self):
```

```
        print("Car is honking.")
```

```
car = Car()
car.move()  # Output: Vehicle is moving.
car.honk()  # Output: Car is honking.
```

- **Java**:

java

```java
class Vehicle {
    public void move() {
        System.out.println("Vehicle is moving.");
    }
}

class Car extends Vehicle {
    public void honk() {
        System.out.println("Car is honking.");
    }
}

public class Main {
    public static void main(String[] args) {
        Car car = new Car();
        car.move();  // Output: Vehicle is moving.
```

```
        car.honk();  // Output: Car is honking.
    }
}
```

11.2.2 Polymorphism

Polymorphism allows methods to have different behaviors depending on the object calling them.

- **Example**: A start method behaves differently for a Car and a Bike.
- **Python**:

python

```python
class Car:
    def start(self):
        print("Car is starting.")

class Bike:
    def start(self):
        print("Bike is starting.")

def start_vehicle(vehicle):
    vehicle.start()
```

```
start_vehicle(Car())  # Output: Car is starting.
start_vehicle(Bike())  # Output: Bike is starting.
```

- **Java**:

```java
class Vehicle {
    public void start() {
        System.out.println("Vehicle is starting.");
    }
}

class Car extends Vehicle {
    public void start() {
        System.out.println("Car is starting.");
    }
}

class Bike extends Vehicle {
    public void start() {
        System.out.println("Bike is starting.");
    }
}

public class Main {
```

```
public static void main(String[] args) {
    Vehicle car = new Car();
    Vehicle bike = new Bike();
    car.start();  // Output: Car is starting.
    bike.start();  // Output: Bike is starting.
  }
}
```

11.2.3 Encapsulation

Encapsulation restricts direct access to an object's attributes and provides controlled access through methods.

- **Python**:

python

```
class BankAccount:
    def __init__(self):
        self.__balance = 0  # Private attribute

    def deposit(self, amount):
        self.__balance += amount

    def get_balance(self):
        return self.__balance
```

```
account = BankAccount()
account.deposit(100)
print(account.get_balance())  # Output: 100
```

- **Java**:

```java
java

public class BankAccount {
    private double balance;  // Private attribute

    public void deposit(double amount) {
        balance += amount;
    }

    public double getBalance() {
        return balance;
    }

    public static void main(String[] args) {
        BankAccount account = new BankAccount();
        account.deposit(100);
        System.out.println(account.getBalance());   // Output:
100.0
    }
```

```
}
```

11.3 Real-World Example: Designing a Library System

Problem Description

A library system manages books and users. Books have titles and authors, and users can borrow books.

11.3.1 Python Implementation

python

```python
class Book:
    def __init__(self, title, author):
        self.title = title
        self.author = author
        self.is_borrowed = False

    def borrow(self):
        if not self.is_borrowed:
            self.is_borrowed = True
            return f"You borrowed {self.title}."
        return f"{self.title} is already borrowed."

    def return_book(self):
```

```python
        self.is_borrowed = False
        return f"You returned {self.title}."


class Library:
    def __init__(self):
        self.books = []

    def add_book(self, book):
        self.books.append(book)

    def list_books(self):
        for book in self.books:
            status = "Available" if not book.is_borrowed else "Borrowed"
            print(f"{book.title} by {book.author} - {status}")


# Example usage
library = Library()
book1 = Book("1984", "George Orwell")
book2 = Book("To Kill a Mockingbird", "Harper Lee")

library.add_book(book1)
library.add_book(book2)
```

```
library.list_books()
print(book1.borrow())
library.list_books()
```

11.3.2 Java Implementation

java

```java
import java.util.ArrayList;

class Book {
    String title;
    String author;
    boolean isBorrowed;

    public Book(String title, String author) {
        this.title = title;
        this.author = author;
        this.isBorrowed = false;
    }

    public String borrow() {
        if (!isBorrowed) {
            isBorrowed = true;
            return "You borrowed " + title;
        }
```

```java
    return title + " is already borrowed.";
  }

  public String returnBook() {
    isBorrowed = false;
    return "You returned " + title;
  }
}

class Library {
  ArrayList<Book> books = new ArrayList<>();

  public void addBook(Book book) {
    books.add(book);
  }

  public void listBooks() {
    for (Book book : books) {
      String status = book.isBorrowed ? "Borrowed" : "Available";
      System.out.println(book.title + " by " + book.author + " - " + status);
    }
  }
}
```

```
public class Main {
    public static void main(String[] args) {
        Library library = new Library();
        Book book1 = new Book("1984", "George Orwell");
        Book book2 = new Book("To Kill a Mockingbird", "Harper Lee");

        library.addBook(book1);
        library.addBook(book2);
        library.listBooks();

        System.out.println(book1.borrow());
        library.listBooks();
    }
}
```

11.4 Best Practices in OOP

1. **Use Descriptive Class Names**:
   - Names should reflect their purpose, e.g., Library, Book.
2. **Encapsulate Data**:
   - Use private attributes with getter and setter methods.
3. **Favor Composition Over Inheritance**:

o Use inheritance sparingly to avoid complex hierarchies.

Object-Oriented Programming (OOP) organizes code around classes and objects, enabling modularity, reusability, and scalability. In this chapter, you learned about key OOP principles—inheritance, polymorphism, and encapsulation—and applied them to a real-world library management system. OOP is a cornerstone of modern software development and a critical skill for building robust applications.

In the next chapter, we'll delve into **file handling**, learning how to read, write, and manipulate files in Python and Java. Let's continue coding!

CHAPTER 12: FILE HANDLING

File handling is a crucial programming skill that allows you to read from and write to files. It's used for tasks such as saving logs, storing data persistently, or processing files dynamically. In this chapter, we'll cover:

- Reading and writing files in **Python** and **Java**.

- Handling exceptions during file operations to ensure reliability.
- A real-world example: Creating a simple logging system.

12.1 Reading and Writing Files

12.1.1 File Operations Overview

There are three primary file operations:

1. **Reading**: Extracting data from a file.
2. **Writing**: Overwriting a file with new data.
3. **Appending**: Adding new data to an existing file.

12.1.2 File Handling in Python

Python's built-in open() function is used for file operations.

- **Modes**:
    - "r": Read (default mode).
    - "w": Write (overwrites the file).
    - "a": Append (adds data to the end).
    - "r+": Read and write.

Example:

python

```python
# Writing to a file
with open("example.txt", "w") as file:
    file.write("Hello, World!\n")

# Reading from a file
with open("example.txt", "r") as file:
    content = file.read()
    print(content)

# Appending to a file
with open("example.txt", "a") as file:
    file.write("This is an appended line.\n")
```

12.1.3 File Handling in Java

In Java, file handling is done using classes from the java.io package.

Example:

java

```java
import java.io.*;

public class FileHandling {
    public static void main(String[] args) {
```

```java
// Writing to a file
try (FileWriter writer = new FileWriter("example.txt")) {
    writer.write("Hello, World!\n");
} catch (IOException e) {
    System.out.println("An error occurred: " + e.getMessage());
}


// Reading from a file
try (BufferedReader reader = new BufferedReader(new FileReader("example.txt"))) {
    String line;
    while ((line = reader.readLine()) != null) {
        System.out.println(line);
    }
} catch (IOException e) {
    System.out.println("An error occurred: " + e.getMessage());
}


// Appending to a file
try (FileWriter writer = new FileWriter("example.txt", true)) {
    writer.write("This is an appended line.\n");
} catch (IOException e) {
    System.out.println("An error occurred: " + e.getMessage());
}
}
```

}

12.2 Handling Exceptions During File Operations

File operations are prone to errors, such as missing files or permission issues. Exception handling ensures your program responds gracefully to such errors.

12.2.1 Exception Handling in Python

Use try-except blocks to handle file-related errors.

Example:

python

```
try:
    with open("nonexistent.txt", "r") as file:
        content = file.read()
        print(content)
except FileNotFoundError:
    print("Error: File not found.")
except IOError as e:
    print(f"IO error occurred: {e}")
```

12.2.2 Exception Handling in Java

Use try-catch blocks to handle exceptions like FileNotFoundException and IOException.

Example:

java

```java
import java.io.*;

public class ExceptionHandling {
    public static void main(String[] args) {
        try (BufferedReader reader = new BufferedReader(new FileReader("nonexistent.txt"))) {
            String line;
            while ((line = reader.readLine()) != null) {
                System.out.println(line);
            }
        } catch (FileNotFoundException e) {
            System.out.println("Error: File not found.");
        } catch (IOException e) {
            System.out.println("IO error occurred: " + e.getMessage());
        }
    }
}
```

12.3 Real-World Example: Creating a Simple Logging System

Logging is essential for tracking application behavior, debugging, and error management. Let's build a logging system that writes messages to a log file.

12.3.1 Python Logging System

1. Define a function to log messages.
2. Write logs with timestamps.

Python Code:

python

```
import datetime

def log_message(message, log_file="app.log"):
    with open(log_file, "a") as file:
        timestamp = datetime.datetime.now().strftime("%Y-%m-%d %H:%M:%S")
        file.write(f"[{timestamp}] {message}\n")

# Example usage
log_message("Application started.")
log_message("User logged in.")
```

log_message("An error occurred.")

Generated Log File (app.log):

csharp

[2024-11-21 12:00:00] Application started.

[2024-11-21 12:01:00] User logged in.

[2024-11-21 12:02:00] An error occurred.

12.3.2 Java Logging System

1. Create a method to log messages.
2. Write logs with timestamps.

Java Code:

java

```
import java.io.*;
import java.text.SimpleDateFormat;
import java.util.Date;

public class LoggingSystem {

    public static void logMessage(String message, String logFile) {
        try (FileWriter writer = new FileWriter(logFile, true)) {
```

```java
    String timestamp = new SimpleDateFormat("yyyy-MM-dd
HH:mm:ss").format(new Date());
    writer.write("[" + timestamp + "] " + message + "\n");
  } catch (IOException e) {
    System.out.println("Error writing to log file: " +
e.getMessage());
  }
}

public static void main(String[] args) {
  logMessage("Application started.", "app.log");
  logMessage("User logged in.", "app.log");
  logMessage("An error occurred.", "app.log");
}
}
```

Generated Log File (app.log):

csharp

[2024-11-21 12:00:00] Application started.

[2024-11-21 12:01:00] User logged in.

[2024-11-21 12:02:00] An error occurred.

12.4 Best Practices for File Handling

1. **Use Context Managers**:
   - In Python, use with open() to ensure files are properly closed.
   - In Java, use try-with-resources for automatic resource management.

2. **Check File Existence**:
   - Verify if a file exists before reading or appending.

3. **Handle Errors Gracefully**:
   - Use descriptive error messages in exception handling.

4. **Avoid Hardcoding Paths**:
   - Use relative paths or configuration files to manage file locations.

5. **Secure File Access**:
   - Validate input paths to prevent unauthorized file access.

File handling enables programs to interact with external files for reading, writing, and appending data. In this chapter, you learned how to handle files in Python and Java, manage exceptions, and implement a logging system to track application events. Mastering file operations is essential for building robust and reliable applications.

In the next chapter, we'll explore **recursion**, a powerful technique for solving problems by breaking them into smaller subproblems. Let's continue coding!

CHAPTER 13: RECURSION

Recursion is a powerful programming technique where a function calls itself to solve a problem. This approach is useful for problems that can be broken down into smaller, similar subproblems. In this chapter, we'll explore:

- The concept of recursive functions.
- Comparing recursion in **Python** and **Java**, including stack behavior and recursion limits.
- Real-world examples: Calculating factorials and Fibonacci sequences.

13.1 Understanding Recursive Functions

13.1.1 What is Recursion?

Recursion occurs when a function calls itself to solve smaller instances of the same problem. Each recursive call should bring the problem closer to a base case, which stops the recursion.

13.1.2 Anatomy of a Recursive Function

1. **Base Case**:
   o The condition where recursion stops.
2. **Recursive Case**:
   o The part of the function that reduces the problem and calls itself.

Example: Summing Numbers from 1 to n

- **Recursive Formula**: sum(n) = n + sum(n-1) where sum(1) = 1 (base case).
- **Python**:

python

```python
def sum_recursive(n):
    if n == 1:  # Base case
        return 1
    return n + sum_recursive(n - 1)  # Recursive case


print(sum_recursive(5))  # Output: 15
```

- **Java**:

java

```java
public class RecursionExample {
    public static int sumRecursive(int n) {
        if (n == 1) {  // Base case
            return 1;
        }
        return n + sumRecursive(n - 1);  // Recursive case
    }
```

```
public static void main(String[] args) {
    System.out.println(sumRecursive(5)); // Output: 15
}
}
```

13.1.3 Key Characteristics of Recursion

- **Problem Simplification**: Each recursive call simplifies the problem.
- **Stack Behavior**: Recursive calls are added to the call stack and removed once they return a result.
- **Base Case Importance**: Without a base case, recursion results in infinite calls and stack overflow.

13.2 Python vs. Java: Stack Behavior and Recursion Limits

13.2.1 Stack Behavior in Recursion

- Each function call is stored on the **call stack**, a data structure that tracks active function calls.
- The **last-in, first-out** (LIFO) nature of the call stack ensures the most recent call is resolved first.

Example: For sum_recursive(3), the call stack evolves as:

css

Call Stack:

1. sum_recursive(3) -> returns 3 + sum_recursive(2)

2. sum_recursive(2) -> returns 2 + sum_recursive(1)

3. sum_recursive(1) -> returns 1

Final result: 3 + 2 + 1 = 6.

13.2.2 Recursion Limits

Both Python and Java impose limits to prevent infinite recursion:

- **Python**:
    - The recursion depth limit is set by default (usually 1,000).
    - You can adjust it using sys.setrecursionlimit(), though it risks a crash.

    python

    import sys
    sys.setrecursionlimit(1500)

- **Java**:
    - The stack size is controlled by the JVM (-Xss option).
    - Exceeding the limit results in a StackOverflowError.

Handling Deep Recursion:

- Rewrite the algorithm iteratively if recursion depth is too high.
- Use memoization or dynamic programming for problems like Fibonacci.

13.3 Real-World Examples: Factorials and Fibonacci Sequences

13.3.1 Calculating Factorials

Factorial Definition:

- $n! = n * (n-1) * (n-2) * \ldots * 1$
- Base case: $0! = 1$.

Python:

python

```
def factorial(n):
    if n == 0:  # Base case
        return 1
    return n * factorial(n - 1)  # Recursive case


print(factorial(5))  # Output: 120
```

Java:

java

```java
public class Factorial {
    public static int factorial(int n) {
        if (n == 0) {  // Base case
            return 1;
        }
        return n * factorial(n - 1);  // Recursive case
    }

    public static void main(String[] args) {
        System.out.println(factorial(5));  // Output: 120
    }
}
```

13.3.2 Calculating Fibonacci Sequences

Fibonacci Definition:

- $F(0) = 0, F(1) = 1$
- $F(n) = F(n-1) + F(n-2)$.

Python:

python

```python
def fibonacci(n):
    if n == 0:  # Base case
        return 0
    if n == 1:  # Base case
        return 1
    return fibonacci(n - 1) + fibonacci(n - 2)  # Recursive case


print(fibonacci(6))  # Output: 8
```

Java:

java

```java
public class Fibonacci {
    public static int fibonacci(int n) {
        if (n == 0) {  // Base case
            return 0;
        }
        if (n == 1) {  // Base case
            return 1;
        }
        return fibonacci(n - 1) + fibonacci(n - 2);  // Recursive case
    }

    public static void main(String[] args) {
        System.out.println(fibonacci(6));  // Output: 8
```

}

}

13.3.3 Optimizing Recursive Fibonacci with Memoization

Recursive Fibonacci can be inefficient due to redundant calculations. Memoization stores previously computed results for reuse.

Python:

python

```python
def fibonacci_memo(n, memo={}):
    if n in memo:
        return memo[n]
    if n == 0 or n == 1:
        return n
    memo[n] = fibonacci_memo(n - 1, memo) + fibonacci_memo(n - 2, memo)
    return memo[n]

print(fibonacci_memo(50))  # Output: 12586269025
```

Java:

java

```java
import java.util.HashMap;

public class FibonacciMemo {
    private static HashMap<Integer, Long> memo = new HashMap<>();

    public static long fibonacciMemo(int n) {
        if (memo.containsKey(n)) {
            return memo.get(n);
        }
        if (n == 0 || n == 1) {
            return n;
        }
        long result = fibonacciMemo(n - 1) + fibonacciMemo(n - 2);
        memo.put(n, result);
        return result;
    }

    public static void main(String[] args) {
        System.out.println(fibonacciMemo(50));      // Output: 12586269025
    }
}
```

13.4 Best Practices for Recursion

1. **Ensure a Base Case**:
   o Always define a condition where recursion stops.
2. **Use Iterative Solutions When Depth is High**:
   o Iterative solutions prevent stack overflow.
3. **Optimize with Memoization**:
   o Avoid redundant calculations for overlapping subproblems.
4. **Analyze Complexity**:
   o Be aware of time and space complexity, especially for deep recursion.

Recursion simplifies problems by breaking them into smaller subproblems. In this chapter, you learned about recursive functions, stack behavior, and how to manage recursion limits in Python and Java. Through real-world examples like factorials and Fibonacci sequences, you explored the practical applications of recursion and optimization using memoization.

In the next chapter, we'll dive into **multithreading**, learning how to run multiple tasks simultaneously to improve application performance. Let's continue coding!

CHAPTER 14: UNDERSTANDING APIS

APIs (Application Programming Interfaces) are essential for modern programming, enabling applications to communicate and share data. In this chapter, we'll explore:

- What APIs are and why they are crucial for developers.
- How to interact with APIs using **Python** (requests library) and **Java** (HTTPClient).
- A real-world example: Fetching data from a weather API.

14.1 What are APIs and Why They Matter?

14.1.1 Definition of an API

An **API** is a set of rules and protocols that allow one application to interact with another. It serves as a bridge between systems, enabling them to exchange data or functionality.

14.1.2 Why APIs Matter

1. **Data Access**: APIs allow access to third-party data (e.g., weather information, social media updates).
2. **Integration**: They enable seamless integration between services (e.g., payment gateways like PayPal).

3. **Efficiency**: Simplify complex operations by abstracting underlying implementation details.

14.1.3 Types of APIs

1. **RESTful APIs**: Use HTTP protocols, typically JSON or XML for data exchange.
2. **SOAP APIs**: Use XML and are more strict with their structure.
3. **GraphQL APIs**: Allow clients to request only the data they need.

14.1.4 How APIs Work

1. **Request**:
   o A client sends an HTTP request (e.g., GET, POST) to the API endpoint.
   o Example: GET /weather?city=London HTTP/1.1.
2. **Response**:
   o The server processes the request and returns a response (typically JSON).

14.2 Using APIs in Python

Python's requests library simplifies API interactions.

14.2.1 Making GET Requests

Use the requests.get() method to fetch data from an API.

Example:

python

```
import requests

# API endpoint
url = "https://api.openweathermap.org/data/2.5/weather"
params = {
    "q": "London",
    "appid": "your_api_key",
    "units": "metric"
}

response = requests.get(url, params=params)

if response.status_code == 200:
    data = response.json()
    print(data)
else:
    print("Failed to fetch data:", response.status_code)
```

14.2.2 Making POST Requests

Use requests.post() to send data to the server.

Example:

python

import requests

url = "https://example.com/api/create"
data = {"name": "John", "age": 30}

response = requests.post(url, json=data)

if response.status_code == 201:
    print("Resource created successfully")
else:
    print("Error:", response.status_code)

14.3 Using APIs in Java

Java's java.net and java.net.http packages allow API interactions.

14.3.1 Making GET Requests

Use the HttpClient class to send HTTP requests.

Example:

java

```java
import java.net.http.*;
import java.net.URI;

public class WeatherAPI {
    public static void main(String[] args) {
        String url = "https://api.openweathermap.org/data/2.5/weather?q=London&appid=your_api_key&units=metric";

        HttpClient client = HttpClient.newHttpClient();
        HttpRequest request = HttpRequest.newBuilder()
            .uri(URI.create(url))
            .build();

        client.sendAsync(request, HttpResponse.BodyHandlers.ofString())
            .thenApply(HttpResponse::body)
            .thenAccept(System.out::println)
            .join();
    }
}
```

14.3.2 Making POST Requests

Use HttpRequest to send data to an API.

Example:

java

```
import java.net.http.*;
import java.net.URI;

public class PostExample {
    public static void main(String[] args) throws Exception {
        String url = "https://example.com/api/create";
        String json = "{\"name\":\"John\", \"age\":30}";

        HttpClient client = HttpClient.newHttpClient();
        HttpRequest request = HttpRequest.newBuilder()
            .uri(URI.create(url))
            .header("Content-Type", "application/json")
            .POST(HttpRequest.BodyPublishers.ofString(json))
            .build();

        HttpResponse<String> response = client.send(request,
HttpResponse.BodyHandlers.ofString());
        System.out.println(response.body());
    }
}
```

14.4 Real-World Example: Fetching Data from a Weather API

Problem Description

Create a program that fetches and displays the current temperature and weather conditions for a given city.

14.4.1 Python Implementation

python

```python
import requests

def get_weather(city):
    url = "https://api.openweathermap.org/data/2.5/weather"
    params = {
        "q": city,
        "appid": "your_api_key",
        "units": "metric"
    }

    response = requests.get(url, params=params)

    if response.status_code == 200:
        data = response.json()
        weather = data["weather"][0]["description"]
        temperature = data["main"]["temp"]
```

```python
        print(f"Weather in {city}: {weather}, {temperature}°C")
    else:
        print("Failed to fetch weather data:", response.status_code)

# Example usage
get_weather("London")
```

14.4.2 Java Implementation
java

```java
import java.net.http.*;
import java.net.URI;
import org.json.JSONObject;

public class WeatherAPI {
    public static void main(String[] args) {
        String apiKey = "your_api_key";
        String city = "London";
        String url = "https://api.openweathermap.org/data/2.5/weather?q=" + city + "&appid=" + apiKey + "&units=metric";

        HttpClient client = HttpClient.newHttpClient();
        HttpRequest request = HttpRequest.newBuilder()
            .uri(URI.create(url))
```

```
        .build();


    client.sendAsync(request,
HttpResponse.BodyHandlers.ofString())
        .thenApply(HttpResponse::body)
        .thenAccept(response -> {
        JSONObject json = new JSONObject(response);
        String                weather              =
json.getJSONArray("weather").getJSONObject(0).getString("descr
iption");
        double                 temp                 =
json.getJSONObject("main").getDouble("temp");
        System.out.println("Weather in " + city + ": " + weather
+ ", " + temp + "°C");
        })
        .join();
    }
}
```

Output:

arduino

Weather in London: clear sky, 15.0°C

14.5 Best Practices for Using APIs

1. **Handle Errors Gracefully**:
   - Check the HTTP status code (200 for success).
   - Implement retries for temporary errors.

2. **Secure API Keys**:
   - Never hardcode API keys in your source code.
   - Use environment variables or configuration files.

3. **Read Documentation**:
   - Each API has unique endpoints, parameters, and response formats.

4. **Throttle Requests**:
   - Respect rate limits to avoid being blocked.

APIs are a cornerstone of modern development, enabling seamless communication between applications. In this chapter, you learned how to interact with APIs using Python's requests library and Java's HttpClient. Through a real-world example of fetching weather data, you applied these concepts to retrieve and display information dynamically. Mastering APIs is critical for integrating external services and building scalable applications.

In the next chapter, we'll explore **database integration**, learning how to connect Python and Java programs to relational databases for robust data management. Let's keep coding!

CHAPTER 15: DEBUGGING AND ERROR HANDLING

Debugging and error handling are essential skills for identifying, diagnosing, and resolving issues in code. This chapter covers:

- Common errors in **Python** and **Java**.
- Debugging tools and techniques for both languages.
- A real-world example: Debugging a faulty calculator program.

15.1 Common Errors in Python and Java

Errors, or exceptions, occur when a program encounters unexpected conditions. Let's explore some common types of errors.

15.1.1 Common Errors in Python

1. **Syntax Errors**:
   - Occur when the code violates Python's syntax rules.
   - Example:

   python

   if x == 5 # Missing colon

print("x is 5")

2. **Name Errors**:
   - o Occur when a variable or function is used before being defined.
   - o Example:

   python

   print(x) # x is not defined

3. **Type Errors**:
   - o Occur when operations are performed on incompatible data types.
   - o Example:

   python

   print("5" + 5) # Cannot add string and integer

4. **Index Errors**:
   - o Occur when trying to access an invalid index in a list.
   - o Example:

   python

```python
numbers = [1, 2, 3]
print(numbers[5])  # Index out of range
```

5. **Value Errors**:
   - o Occur when an operation receives an argument of the right type but an invalid value.
   - o Example:

   python

   ```python
   int("abc")  # Cannot convert "abc" to integer
   ```

15.1.2 Common Errors in Java

1. **Syntax Errors**:
   - o Similar to Python, Java syntax errors occur when the code doesn't follow the language rules.
   - o Example:

   java

   ```java
   if (x == 5)  // Missing curly braces
   System.out.println("x is 5");
   ```

2. **Null Pointer Exception**:

- Occurs when trying to use an object that has not been initialized.
- Example:

java

```
String str = null;
System.out.println(str.length());        //
NullPointerException
```

3. **Array Index Out of Bounds**:
   - Occurs when accessing an invalid index in an array.
   - Example:

java

```
int[] numbers = {1, 2, 3};
System.out.println(numbers[5]);        //
IndexOutOfBoundsException
```

4. **ClassCastException**:
   - Occurs when trying to cast an object to an incompatible type.
   - Example:

java

Object obj = "Hello";

Integer num = (Integer) obj; // ClassCastException

5. **ArithmeticException**:
   - o Occurs during illegal arithmetic operations like division by zero.
   - o Example:

   java

   int result = 10 / 0; // ArithmeticException

15.2 Debugging Tools and Techniques

15.2.1 Debugging Tools in Python

1. **Print Statements**:
   - o Add print() statements to track variable values.
   - o Example:

   python

   x = 10
   print("x =", x)

2. **Python Debugger (pdb)**:
   - o A built-in debugger for step-by-step execution.

- o Example:

python

import pdb
pdb.set_trace()
x = 10
y = x + 5
print(y)

3. **Integrated Development Environments (IDEs)**:
    - o Use IDEs like PyCharm or VS Code for breakpoints and variable inspection.

15.2.2 Debugging Tools in Java

1. **Print Statements**:
    - o Use System.out.println() to display variable values.
    - o Example:

java

int x = 10;
System.out.println("x = " + x);

2. **Java Debugger (jdb)**:

o A command-line tool for debugging Java programs.

3. **IDE Debugging**:

   o Use IDEs like IntelliJ IDEA or Eclipse for:

     ▪ Setting breakpoints.

     ▪ Stepping through code.

     ▪ Inspecting variables.

4. **Logging Frameworks**:

   o Use libraries like Log4j or SLF4J for structured logging.

15.2.3 General Debugging Techniques

1. **Reproduce the Bug**:

   o Ensure the issue is consistently reproducible.

2. **Isolate the Problem**:

   o Narrow down the code section causing the bug.

3. **Read Error Messages**:

   o Analyze stack traces and error messages for clues.

4. **Test Incrementally**:

   o Test small sections of code before running the entire program.

5. **Rubber Duck Debugging**:

   o Explain the problem to someone (or an inanimate object) to gain clarity.

15.3 Real-World Example: Debugging a Faulty Calculator Program

15.3.1 Problem Description

The calculator program is supposed to perform basic arithmetic operations. However, it produces incorrect results for some inputs. Debug and fix the issues.

15.3.2 Python Implementation

Faulty Code:

python

```python
def add(a, b):
    return a - b  # Error: Subtraction instead of addition

def divide(a, b):
    return a / b  # Missing check for division by zero

# Testing the calculator
print(add(5, 3))  # Expected: 8, Output: 2
print(divide(10, 0))   # Expected: Error handling, Output: ZeroDivisionError
```

Debugging and Fixing:

1. Use print statements to identify incorrect logic.
2. Add error handling for division.

Corrected Code:

python

```python
def add(a, b):
    return a + b  # Fixed addition logic

def divide(a, b):
    if b == 0:
        return "Error: Division by zero"  # Added error handling
    return a / b

# Testing the calculator
print(add(5, 3))  # Output: 8
print(divide(10, 0))  # Output: Error: Division by zero
```

15.3.3 Java Implementation
Faulty Code:

java

```java
public class Calculator {
    public static int add(int a, int b) {
```

```java
    return a - b;  // Error: Subtraction instead of addition
  }

  public static int divide(int a, int b) {
    return a / b;  // Missing check for division by zero
  }

  public static void main(String[] args) {
    System.out.println(add(5, 3));  // Expected: 8, Output: 2
    System.out.println(divide(10,  0));     //  Expected:  Error
handling, Output: ArithmeticException
  }
}
```

Debugging and Fixing:

1. Analyze error messages for incorrect logic.
2. Add exception handling for division.

Corrected Code:

java

```java
public class Calculator {
  public static int add(int a, int b) {
    return a + b; // Fixed addition logic
  }
```

```java
public static String divide(int a, int b) {
    if (b == 0) {
        return "Error: Division by zero";  // Added error handling
    }
    return String.valueOf(a / b);
}

public static void main(String[] args) {
    System.out.println(add(5, 3));  // Output: 8
    System.out.println(divide(10, 0));  // Output: Error: Division by zero
    }
}
```

15.4 Best Practices for Debugging and Error Handling

1. **Anticipate Common Errors**:
   - o Validate input and handle edge cases.
2. **Write Readable Code**:
   - o Easier-to-read code is easier to debug.
3. **Log Errors**:
   - o Use structured logging for detailed error reports.
4. **Use Unit Tests**:
   - o Write tests to catch bugs early.

5. **Fail Gracefully**:

   o Ensure the program doesn't crash on unexpected inputs.

Debugging and error handling are integral to developing robust software. In this chapter, you explored common errors in Python and Java, learned about debugging tools like pdb and IDE breakpoints, and applied these techniques to fix a faulty calculator program. Mastering these skills ensures your code is resilient and maintainable.

In the next chapter, we'll explore **data visualization**, learning how to create insightful visual representations of data using libraries in Python and Java. Let's continue coding!

CHAPTER 16: INTRODUCTION TO DATABASES

Databases are an essential tool for storing, organizing, and retrieving data efficiently. In this chapter, you'll learn about:

- Relational databases and their structure.
- Basic SQL operations like queries, tables, and joins.
- A real-world example: Storing and managing user profiles in a MySQL database.

16.1 Understanding Relational Databases

16.1.1 What is a Relational Database?

A relational database is a structured collection of data organized into tables. Each table consists of rows and columns:

- **Rows** represent individual records.
- **Columns** represent attributes or fields.

16.1.2 Key Concepts

1. **Tables**:

- Core structures in a database.
- Example:

ID Name Email

1   Alice   alice@example.com

2   Bob   bob@example.com

2. **Primary Key**:
   - A unique identifier for each record in a table.
3. **Foreign Key**:
   - A field in one table that links to the primary key of another table.
4. **Relationships**:
   - **One-to-One**: A row in Table A relates to one row in Table B.
   - **One-to-Many**: A row in Table A relates to many rows in Table B.
   - **Many-to-Many**: Rows in Table A relate to many rows in Table B via a junction table.

16.2 SQL Basics: Queries, Tables, and Joins

16.2.1 What is SQL?

SQL (Structured Query Language) is used to interact with relational databases. Common SQL operations include:

- **CRUD**: Create, Read, Update, Delete.
- **DDL**: Data Definition Language (e.g., CREATE, ALTER).
- **DML**: Data Manipulation Language (e.g., INSERT, SELECT).

16.2.2 Creating and Managing Tables

Creating a Table:

sql

```
CREATE TABLE Users (
    ID INT AUTO_INCREMENT PRIMARY KEY,
    Name VARCHAR(100),
    Email VARCHAR(100)
);
```

Inserting Data:

sql

```
INSERT INTO Users (Name, Email) VALUES ('Alice', 'alice@example.com');
```

INSERT INTO Users (Name, Email) VALUES ('Bob', 'bob@example.com');

Querying Data:

sql

SELECT * FROM Users;

Output:

ID Name Email

1   Alice   alice@example.com

2   Bob   bob@example.com

16.2.3 Joining Tables

Joins combine data from multiple tables based on a related column.

Example:

sql

SELECT Users.Name, Orders.OrderDate
FROM Users
INNER JOIN Orders ON Users.ID = Orders.UserID;

16.3 Real-World Example: Storing User Profiles in MySQL

16.3.1 Problem Description

Design a database to store user profiles, including personal details and account activity.

16.3.2 Setting Up the Database

1. **Users Table**:
   o Stores user details.

   sql

   ```
   CREATE TABLE Users (
       ID INT AUTO_INCREMENT PRIMARY KEY,
       Name VARCHAR(100),
       Email VARCHAR(100)
   );
   ```

2. **Activity Table**:
   o Tracks user activity.

   sql

   ```
   CREATE TABLE Activity (
       ID INT AUTO_INCREMENT PRIMARY KEY,
       UserID INT,
       Action VARCHAR(255),
   ```

```
            Timestamp DATETIME,
            FOREIGN KEY (UserID) REFERENCES Users(ID)
       );
```

16.3.3 Managing Data

Inserting Users:

sql

```sql
INSERT INTO Users (Name, Email) VALUES ('Alice',
'alice@example.com');
INSERT INTO Users (Name, Email) VALUES ('Bob',
'bob@example.com');
```

Inserting Activities:

sql

```sql
INSERT INTO Activity (UserID, Action, Timestamp)
VALUES (1, 'Logged in', NOW());
INSERT INTO Activity (UserID, Action, Timestamp)
VALUES (2, 'Uploaded a file', NOW());
```

Querying User Profiles:

sql

```sql
SELECT Users.Name, Activity.Action, Activity.Timestamp
FROM Users
```

INNER JOIN Activity ON Users.ID = Activity.UserID;

Output:

Name	Action	Timestamp
Alice	Logged in	2024-11-21 12:00:00
Bob	Uploaded a file	2024-11-21 12:05:00

16.4 Using Python and Java for Database Interaction

16.4.1 Python: Connecting to MySQL

Use the mysql-connector-python library for MySQL interaction.

Installation:

bash

```
pip install mysql-connector-python
```

Code Example:

python

```
import mysql.connector

# Connect to the database
db = mysql.connector.connect(
```

```python
    host="localhost",
    user="root",
    password="password",
    database="test_db"
)

cursor = db.cursor()

# Query data
cursor.execute("SELECT Name, Email FROM Users")
for name, email in cursor.fetchall():
    print(f"{name}: {email}")
```

16.4.2 Java: Connecting to MySQL

Use the JDBC library for database interaction.

Code Example:

java

```java
import java.sql.*;

public class DatabaseExample {
    public static void main(String[] args) {
        String url = "jdbc:mysql://localhost:3306/test_db";
        String user = "root";
```

```
String password = "password";

try (Connection  conn  =  DriverManager.getConnection(url,
user, password)) {
    Statement stmt = conn.createStatement();
    ResultSet rs = stmt.executeQuery("SELECT Name, Email
FROM Users");

    while (rs.next()) {
        System.out.println(rs.getString("Name")  +  ":  "  +
rs.getString("Email"));
    }
} catch (SQLException e) {
    e.printStackTrace();
}
}
}
```

16.5 Best Practices for Databases

1. **Normalize Your Database**:
    o Avoid redundancy by structuring tables efficiently.
2. **Use Indexing**:
    o Speed up searches with indexed columns.
3. **Secure Connections**:

- o Use encrypted connections and secure credentials.
4. **Back Up Regularly**:
    - o Prevent data loss with frequent backups.
5. **Avoid SQL Injection**:
    - o Use parameterized queries to prevent attacks.

Relational databases provide a structured way to store and retrieve data efficiently. In this chapter, you learned the basics of SQL, including creating tables, inserting data, and using joins to combine information. The real-world example of managing user profiles demonstrated how relational databases power applications. You also explored how to interact with databases using Python and Java.

In the next chapter, we'll dive into **web development fundamentals**, where we'll explore how to build dynamic web applications. Let's continue coding!

CHAPTER 17: BUILDING A SIMPLE WEB APPLICATION

Web applications are dynamic programs that run on web browsers, enabling users to interact with content and logic over the internet. In this chapter, we'll cover:

- An introduction to web technologies: **HTML**, **CSS**, and either **Flask** (Python) or **Spring** (Java).
- Connecting the front-end (user interface) with back-end logic (server-side processing).
- A real-world example: Building a **to-do list web application**.

17.1 Introduction to Web Technologies

Web development involves three main components:

1. **HTML (HyperText Markup Language)**:
   - Defines the structure of a web page.
2. **CSS (Cascading Style Sheets)**:

     o Adds styling to the web page (e.g., colors, fonts).

3. **JavaScript (Optional for this example)**:

     o Adds interactivity (e.g., dynamic forms, animations).

17.1.1 Example: A Basic HTML Page

html

```html
<!DOCTYPE html>
<html>
<head>
  <title>To-Do List</title>
  <style>
    body { font-family: Arial, sans-serif; }
    h1 { color: blue; }
  </style>
</head>
<body>
  <h1>My To-Do List</h1>
  <ul>
    <li>Learn Python</li>
    <li>Build a Web App</li>
  </ul>
</body>
</html>
```

17.2 Introduction to Flask (Python)

Flask is a lightweight framework for building web applications in Python.

17.2.1 Setting Up Flask

1. Install Flask:

   bash

   ```
   pip install flask
   ```

2. Create a basic Flask app:

   python

   ```
   from flask import Flask

   app = Flask(__name__)

   @app.route("/")
   def home():
       return "<h1>Welcome to My To-Do List</h1>"

   if __name__ == "__main__":
       app.run(debug=True)
   ```

17.3 Introduction to Spring (Java)

Spring Boot is a framework for building robust web applications in Java.

17.3.1 Setting Up Spring Boot

1. Use Spring Initializr to create a new project:
   - Go to https://start.spring.io.
   - Add dependencies: Spring Web, Thymeleaf.
2. Create a basic Spring Boot app:

java

```
import org.springframework.boot.SpringApplication;
import org.springframework.boot.autoconfigure.SpringBootApplication;
import org.springframework.web.bind.annotation.GetMapping;
import org.springframework.web.bind.annotation.RestController;

@SpringBootApplication
public class ToDoApp {
    public static void main(String[] args) {
        SpringApplication.run(ToDoApp.class, args);
```

```
        }
    }


    @RestController
    class ToDoController {
      @GetMapping("/")
      public String home() {
          return "<h1>Welcome to My To-Do List</h1>";
      }
    }
```

17.4 Connecting the Front-End with Back-End Logic

To create a complete application, the front-end (HTML/CSS) must communicate with the back-end (Flask or Spring).

17.4.1 Flask Example
Directory Structure:

lua

project/
|-- app.py
|-- templates/
    |-- index.html

Flask Code:

python

```python
from flask import Flask, render_template, request

app = Flask(__name__)

# Store tasks in a list
tasks = []

@app.route("/")
def home():
    return render_template("index.html", tasks=tasks)

@app.route("/add", methods=["POST"])
def add_task():
    task = request.form["task"]
    tasks.append(task)
    return render_template("index.html", tasks=tasks)

if __name__ == "__main__":
    app.run(debug=True)
```

HTML Code (templates/index.html):

html

```html
<!DOCTYPE html>
```

```
<html>
<head>
  <title>To-Do List</title>
</head>
<body>
  <h1>To-Do List</h1>
  <form method="post" action="/add">
    <input type="text" name="task" placeholder="Enter a task"
required>
    <button type="submit">Add Task</button>
  </form>
  <ul>
    {% for task in tasks %}
      <li>{{ task }}</li>
    {% endfor %}
  </ul>
</body>
</html>
```

17.4.2 Spring Example

Directory Structure:

lua

src/main/

```
|-- java/
|   |-- com.example.todo/
|       |-- ToDoApp.java
|       |-- ToDoController.java
|-- resources/
    |-- templates/
        |-- index.html
```

Spring Controller Code (ToDoController.java):

java

```java
import org.springframework.stereotype.Controller;
import org.springframework.ui.Model;
import org.springframework.web.bind.annotation.GetMapping;
import org.springframework.web.bind.annotation.PostMapping;
import org.springframework.web.bind.annotation.RequestParam;

import java.util.ArrayList;
import java.util.List;

@Controller
public class ToDoController {
    private List<String> tasks = new ArrayList<>();

    @GetMapping("/")
    public String home(Model model) {
```

```
    model.addAttribute("tasks", tasks);
    return "index";
  }


  @PostMapping("/add")
  public String addTask(@RequestParam String task, Model
model) {
    tasks.add(task);
    model.addAttribute("tasks", tasks);
    return "index";
  }
}
```

HTML Code (resources/templates/index.html):

html

```html
<!DOCTYPE html>
<html>
<head>
  <title>To-Do List</title>
</head>
<body>
  <h1>To-Do List</h1>
  <form method="post" action="/add">
    <input type="text" name="task" placeholder="Enter a task"
required>
```

```
    <button type="submit">Add Task</button>
  </form>
  <ul>
    <th:block th:each="task : ${tasks}">
      <li th:text="${task}"></li>
    </th:block>
  </ul>
</body>
</html>
```

17.5 Real-World Example: A To-Do List Web Application

Features of the To-Do App:

1. Add tasks dynamically.
2. Display the list of tasks.
3. Provide a user-friendly interface.

17.5.1 Python Flask Example Output:

1. **Homepage**:
    o Displays a form and current tasks.
2. **Adding a Task**:
    o Submits the task to the server, updates the task list.

17.5.2 Java Spring Example Output:

1. **Homepage**:
   - Renders tasks using Thymeleaf templating.
2. **Adding a Task**:
   - Handles form submission via POST and updates the task list dynamically.

17.6 Best Practices for Web Development

1. **Separate Concerns**:
   - Use templates for front-end and controllers for back-end logic.
2. **Validate Input**:
   - Validate user input on both client-side (JavaScript) and server-side.
3. **Use Framework Tools**:
   - Leverage features of Flask (e.g., render_template) and Spring (e.g., Thymeleaf).
4. **Secure Applications**:
   - Avoid exposing sensitive data and use HTTPS for production environments.

Building a web application involves combining front-end technologies (HTML, CSS) with back-end frameworks like Flask or Spring. In this chapter, you built a dynamic to-do list application, learning how to connect user interfaces to back-end logic. This foundational knowledge prepares you to tackle more complex web development projects.

In the next chapter, we'll explore **data visualization**, learning how to present insights effectively using libraries in Python and Java. Let's continue coding!

CHAPTER 18: INTRODUCTION TO DATA ANALYSIS

Data analysis is a key skill in understanding patterns, trends, and insights from raw data. In this chapter, you'll explore:

- Using Python libraries like **pandas** and **matplotlib** for data analysis and visualization.
- Java's data analysis capabilities using **Apache Commons Math**.
- A real-world example: Visualizing sales data.

18.1 Python for Data Analysis

Python is widely used in data analysis due to its rich ecosystem of libraries like pandas (data manipulation) and matplotlib (visualization).

18.1.1 Using pandas

pandas is a library for manipulating and analyzing structured data, such as tables or spreadsheets.

Installation:

bash

pip install pandas

Example: Loading and Manipulating Data:

python

```python
import pandas as pd

# Sample sales data
data = {
    "Date": ["2024-01-01", "2024-01-02", "2024-01-03"],
    "Product": ["A", "B", "A"],
    "Sales": [100, 200, 150]
}

# Create a DataFrame
df = pd.DataFrame(data)

# View the data
print(df)

# Summarize total sales by product
sales_summary = df.groupby("Product")["Sales"].sum()
print(sales_summary)
```

Output:

css

```
     Date Product  Sales
0  2024-01-01   A    100
1  2024-01-02   B    200
2  2024-01-03   A    150
```

```
Product
A    250
B    200
Name: Sales, dtype: int64
```

18.1.2 Visualizing Data with matplotlib

matplotlib is a versatile library for creating static, animated, and interactive plots.

Installation:

bash

```bash
pip install matplotlib
```

Example: Visualizing Sales:

python

```python
import matplotlib.pyplot as plt
```

```
# Visualize sales summary
sales_summary.plot(kind="bar")
plt.title("Total Sales by Product")
plt.xlabel("Product")
plt.ylabel("Sales")
plt.show()
```

Output: A bar chart showing total sales for each product.

18.2 Java for Data Analysis

Java has fewer dedicated libraries for data analysis compared to Python but is still capable using tools like **Apache Commons Math** for mathematical computations.

18.2.1 Using Apache Commons Math

Apache Commons Math provides utilities for statistical and mathematical operations.

Setup: Add the dependency to your pom.xml if using Maven:

xml

```xml
<dependency>
    <groupId>org.apache.commons</groupId>
    <artifactId>commons-math3</artifactId>
    <version>3.6.1</version>
```

</dependency>

Example: Calculating Sales Statistics:

java

```java
import
org.apache.commons.math3.stat.descriptive.DescriptiveStatistics;

public class SalesAnalysis {
    public static void main(String[] args) {
        // Sample sales data
        double[] sales = {100, 200, 150};

        // Calculate statistics
        DescriptiveStatistics stats = new DescriptiveStatistics();
        for (double sale : sales) {
            stats.addValue(sale);
        }

        System.out.println("Mean Sales: " + stats.getMean());
        System.out.println("Max Sales: " + stats.getMax());
        System.out.println("Min Sales: " + stats.getMin());
    }
}
```

Output:

mathematica

Mean Sales: 150.0

Max Sales: 200.0

Min Sales: 100.0

18.2.2 Visualizing Data in Java

Java does not have built-in visualization libraries like Python, but you can use **JFreeChart**.

Setup: Add the dependency to your pom.xml:

xml

```
<dependency>
   <groupId>org.jfree</groupId>
   <artifactId>jfreechart</artifactId>
   <version>1.5.3</version>
</dependency>
```

Example: Creating a Bar Chart:

java

```
import org.jfree.chart.ChartFactory;
import org.jfree.chart.ChartPanel;
import org.jfree.chart.JFreeChart;
```

```java
import org.jfree.data.category.DefaultCategoryDataset;

import javax.swing.*;

public class SalesChart {
    public static void main(String[] args) {
        // Create dataset
        DefaultCategoryDataset dataset = new DefaultCategoryDataset();
        dataset.addValue(250, "Sales", "Product A");
        dataset.addValue(200, "Sales", "Product B");

        // Create chart
        JFreeChart chart = ChartFactory.createBarChart(
            "Total Sales by Product", "Product", "Sales", dataset);

        // Display chart in a frame
        JFrame frame = new JFrame();
        frame.setContentPane(new ChartPanel(chart));
        frame.setSize(800, 600);
        frame.setDefaultCloseOperation(JFrame.EXIT_ON_CLOSE);
        frame.setVisible(true);
    }
}
```

Output: A graphical bar chart displaying total sales for each product.

18.3 Real-World Example: Visualizing Sales Data

Problem Description

You're tasked with analyzing and visualizing sales data for products over a given period.

18.3.1 Python Implementation

python

```python
import pandas as pd
import matplotlib.pyplot as plt

# Sample sales data
data = {
    "Date": ["2024-01-01", "2024-01-02", "2024-01-03", "2024-01-04"],
    "Product": ["A", "B", "A", "B"],
    "Sales": [100, 200, 150, 300]
}

# Create a DataFrame
df = pd.DataFrame(data)
```

```python
# Aggregate sales by product
sales_summary = df.groupby("Product")["Sales"].sum()

# Visualize sales summary
sales_summary.plot(kind="bar", color=["blue", "green"])
plt.title("Total Sales by Product")
plt.xlabel("Product")
plt.ylabel("Sales")
plt.show()
```

Output: A bar chart comparing total sales for products A and B.

18.3.2 Java Implementation

java

```java
import org.jfree.chart.ChartFactory;
import org.jfree.chart.ChartPanel;
import org.jfree.chart.JFreeChart;
import org.jfree.data.category.DefaultCategoryDataset;

import javax.swing.*;

public class SalesVisualization {
    public static void main(String[] args) {
```

```
    // Sample sales data
    double productASales = 250;
    double productBSales = 500;

    // Create dataset
    DefaultCategoryDataset        dataset        =        new
DefaultCategoryDataset();
    dataset.addValue(productASales, "Sales", "Product A");
    dataset.addValue(productBSales, "Sales", "Product B");

    // Create chart
    JFreeChart chart = ChartFactory.createBarChart(
        "Total Sales by Product", "Product", "Sales", dataset);

    // Display chart
    JFrame frame = new JFrame("Sales Visualization");
    frame.setContentPane(new ChartPanel(chart));
    frame.setSize(800, 600);
    frame.setDefaultCloseOperation(JFrame.EXIT_ON_CLOSE);
    frame.setVisible(true);
  }
}
```

Output: A bar chart comparing total sales for products A and B.

18.4 Best Practices for Data Analysis

1. **Clean Your Data**:
   - o Remove duplicates, handle missing values, and standardize formats.

2. **Choose the Right Tools**:
   - o Use libraries suited for your needs (e.g., pandas for Python, JFreeChart for Java).

3. **Visualize Insights**:
   - o Use charts to communicate data trends and findings effectively.

4. **Document Your Process**:
   - o Keep track of transformations and assumptions made during analysis.

Data analysis transforms raw data into meaningful insights. In this chapter, you explored Python's pandas and matplotlib libraries and Java's Apache Commons Math and JFreeChart for analysis and visualization. Through the real-world example of sales data visualization, you applied these tools to uncover trends and communicate findings. Mastery of data analysis is a valuable skill across industries.

In the next chapter, we'll dive into **artificial intelligence basics**, introducing concepts and applications of AI with hands-on examples. Let's continue coding!

CHAPTER 19: INTRODUCTION TO MACHINE LEARNING

Machine learning (ML) is a subset of artificial intelligence that enables systems to learn patterns from data and make predictions or decisions without explicit programming. This chapter covers:

- The basics of machine learning, including **supervised** and **unsupervised learning**.
- Practical tools for ML: **scikit-learn** (Python) and **Weka** (Java).
- A real-world example: Predicting house prices.

19.1 Basics of Machine Learning

19.1.1 What is Machine Learning?

Machine learning involves building models that learn from data to perform specific tasks such as classification, regression, clustering, or recommendation.

19.1.2 Types of Machine Learning

1. **Supervised Learning**:
   - o The model learns from labeled data (input-output pairs).
   - o Tasks:
     - **Regression**: Predict a continuous value (e.g., house prices).
     - **Classification**: Predict a category (e.g., spam or not spam).
   - o Example:
     - Input: Features of a house (size, location).
     - Output: House price.

2. **Unsupervised Learning**:
   - o The model learns patterns from unlabeled data.
   - o Tasks:
     - **Clustering**: Group similar data points (e.g., customer segmentation).
     - **Dimensionality Reduction**: Reduce data complexity (e.g., PCA).
   - o Example:
     - Input: Customer purchase data.
     - Output: Groups of similar customers.

19.2 Using scikit-learn (Python)

scikit-learn is a powerful library for machine learning in Python. It provides tools for preprocessing, modeling, and evaluation.

19.2.1 Setting Up scikit-learn

Install the library:

bash

pip install scikit-learn

19.2.2 Building a Supervised Learning Model

Example: Predicting House Prices Using Linear Regression

python

```python
import pandas as pd
from sklearn.model_selection import train_test_split
from sklearn.linear_model import LinearRegression
from sklearn.metrics import mean_squared_error

# Sample data
data = {
```

```python
    "Size (sq ft)": [850, 900, 1000, 1200, 1500],
    "Bedrooms": [2, 2, 3, 3, 4],
    "Price": [300000, 310000, 340000, 400000, 500000]
}

# Load data into a DataFrame
df = pd.DataFrame(data)

# Features (X) and target (y)
X = df[["Size (sq ft)", "Bedrooms"]]
y = df["Price"]

# Split into training and testing sets
X_train, X_test, y_train, y_test = train_test_split(X, y,
test_size=0.2, random_state=42)

# Train a linear regression model
model = LinearRegression()
model.fit(X_train, y_train)

# Make predictions
y_pred = model.predict(X_test)

# Evaluate the model
mse = mean_squared_error(y_test, y_pred)
```

```python
print("Mean Squared Error:", mse)

# Example prediction
new_house = [[1300, 3]]
predicted_price = model.predict(new_house)
print("Predicted Price for 1300 sq ft, 3-bedroom house:",
predicted_price[0])
```

19.3 Using Weka (Java)

Weka is a Java-based software suite for machine learning and data mining.

19.3.1 Setting Up Weka

1. Download Weka: https://www.cs.waikato.ac.nz/ml/weka/.
2. Add Weka to your Java project using Maven:

   xml

```xml
<dependency>
    <groupId>nz.ac.waikato.cms.weka</groupId>
    <artifactId>weka-stable</artifactId>
    <version>3.8.5</version>
</dependency>
```

19.3.2 Building a Supervised Learning Model

Example: Predicting House Prices Using Linear Regression

java

```java
import weka.core.*;
import weka.classifiers.functions.LinearRegression;

public class HousePricePrediction {
    public static void main(String[] args) throws Exception {
        // Create attributes
        Attribute size = new Attribute("Size (sq ft)");
        Attribute bedrooms = new Attribute("Bedrooms");
        Attribute price = new Attribute("Price");

        // Create dataset
        ArrayList<Attribute> attributes = new ArrayList<>();
        attributes.add(size);
        attributes.add(bedrooms);
        attributes.add(price);
        Instances dataset = new Instances("HousePrices", attributes, 0);
        dataset.setClassIndex(2); // Price is the target attribute
```

```
// Add data
double[] instance1 = {850, 2, 300000};
double[] instance2 = {900, 2, 310000};
double[] instance3 = {1000, 3, 340000};
double[] instance4 = {1200, 3, 400000};
double[] instance5 = {1500, 4, 500000};

dataset.add(new DenseInstance(1.0, instance1));
dataset.add(new DenseInstance(1.0, instance2));
dataset.add(new DenseInstance(1.0, instance3));
dataset.add(new DenseInstance(1.0, instance4));
dataset.add(new DenseInstance(1.0, instance5));

// Train linear regression model
LinearRegression model = new LinearRegression();
model.buildClassifier(dataset);

// Predict price for a new house
double[] newHouse = {1300, 3, 0}; // Size, Bedrooms, Price
(unknown)
Instance newInstance = new DenseInstance(1.0, newHouse);
newInstance.setDataset(dataset);

double predictedPrice = model.classifyInstance(newInstance);
```

```
    System.out.println("Predicted Price for 1300 sq ft, 3-bedroom
house: $" + predictedPrice);
    }
}
```

19.4 Real-World Example: Predicting House Prices

Problem Description
Use historical housing data (size, bedrooms, price) to predict the price of a new house.

19.4.1 Python Implementation Output

- **Mean Squared Error**: A numerical value indicating the error between predicted and actual prices.
- **Prediction**:

yaml

Predicted Price for 1300 sq ft, 3-bedroom house: 410000

19.4.2 Java Implementation Output

- **Prediction**:

yaml

Predicted Price for 1300 sq ft, 3-bedroom house: $410000

19.5 Best Practices for Machine Learning

1. **Clean and Prepare Data**:
   - o Handle missing values and outliers before training.
2. **Choose the Right Algorithm**:
   - o Match the algorithm to your problem (e.g., linear regression for regression tasks).
3. **Split Data Properly**:
   - o Use training and testing datasets to evaluate model performance.
4. **Evaluate Models**:
   - o Use metrics like Mean Squared Error (MSE) or Accuracy to assess models.
5. **Avoid Overfitting**:
   - o Regularize models and validate on unseen data.

Machine learning transforms data into actionable insights by building predictive models. In this chapter, you explored supervised and unsupervised learning concepts, implemented a regression model to predict house prices using Python's scikit-learn and Java's Weka, and learned best practices for machine learning projects.

In the next chapter, we'll dive into **networking basics**, exploring how applications communicate over the internet. Let's continue coding!

CHAPTER 20: VERSION CONTROL WITH GIT

Version control systems are essential tools for tracking changes in code, collaborating on projects, and ensuring a clean development workflow. Git is one of the most widely used version control systems. This chapter covers:

- An overview of version control and its importance.
- Git basics: commit, push, pull, and branching.
- A real-world example: Collaborating on a coding project using Git.

20.1 Understanding Version Control

20.1.1 What is Version Control?

Version control is the practice of managing changes to files, typically source code, over time. It allows developers to:

- Track changes to files.
- Revert to previous versions.
- Collaborate with others without overwriting each other's work.

20.1.2 Benefits of Version Control

1. **Collaboration**:
   - Teams can work on the same codebase without conflicts.
2. **Backup**:
   - Changes are stored in a repository, serving as a backup.
3. **History**:
   - Tracks every modification, including who made it and why.
4. **Branching and Merging**:
   - Enables experimentation without affecting the main codebase.

20.2 Git Basics

Git is a distributed version control system, meaning every developer has a full copy of the repository on their machine.

20.2.1 Setting Up Git

1. Install Git:

    o Download from git-scm.com.

2. Configure Git:

bash

git config --global user.name "Your Name"
git config --global user.email "your.email@example.com"

20.2.2 Core Git Commands

1. **Initialize a Repository**:

    o Start tracking a project with Git.

bash

git init

2. **Add Files to Staging**:

    o Prepare files for a commit.

bash

git add <filename>

3. **Commit Changes**:

   o   Save a snapshot of the repository.

bash

git commit -m "Descriptive message"

4. **Check Repository Status**:

   o   See changes that are staged or unstaged.

bash

git status

5. **Push Changes to Remote**:

   o   Upload local commits to a remote repository (e.g., GitHub).

bash

git push origin <branch-name>

6. **Pull Changes from Remote**:

   o   Fetch and merge updates from the remote repository.

bash

git pull origin <branch-name>

20.2.3 Branching and Merging

1. **Create a Branch**:
   - o Branching allows developers to work on features independently.

   bash

   git branch <branch-name>

2. **Switch to a Branch**:

   bash

   git checkout <branch-name>

3. **Merge Branches**:
   - o Combine changes from one branch into another.

   bash

   git merge <branch-name>

4. **Delete a Branch**:

bash

git branch -d <branch-name>

20.3 Real-World Example: Collaborating on a Coding Project

20.3.1 Scenario

A team of developers is collaborating on a web application. Tasks include:

1. Setting up the repository.
2. Working on individual features in branches.
3. Merging the features into the main branch.

20.3.2 Steps

1. **Set Up a Remote Repository**:
   o Create a new repository on GitHub and clone it locally.

bash

```
git clone https://github.com/yourusername/project.git
cd project
```

2. **Initial Commit**:

   o   Add the base project files and make the first commit.

bash

```
git add .
git commit -m "Initial project setup"
git push origin main
```

3. **Create Feature Branches**:

   o   Each developer works on a feature in a separate branch.

bash

```
git checkout -b feature-login
```

4. **Commit Changes in the Feature Branch**:

bash

```
git add login.html
git commit -m "Add login page"
```

5. **Push the Feature Branch**:

bash

git push origin feature-login

6. **Collaborate and Review**:
   o Other team members review the changes using GitHub's pull request feature.
7. **Merge Changes into the Main Branch**:
   o After approval, merge the feature branch.

bash

git checkout main
git merge feature-login
git push origin main

20.3.3 Resolving Conflicts

When two developers modify the same file, Git may encounter a conflict during merging.

Example Conflict:

bash

<<<<<<< HEAD
console.log("Hello from main branch");
=======

console.log("Hello from feature branch");

>>>>>>> feature-login

Resolution: Edit the file to keep the desired changes, then commit the resolved file:

bash

```
git add <filename>
git commit -m "Resolve merge conflict"
```

20.4 Best Practices for Using Git

1. **Write Clear Commit Messages**:
   o Use concise, descriptive messages (e.g., "Fix bug in login validation").
2. **Commit Often**:
   o Make small, frequent commits to track incremental changes.
3. **Use .gitignore**:
   o Exclude unnecessary files (e.g., build files) from version control.

plaintext

```
*.log
node_modules/
```

4. **Pull Before Pushing**:
   - o Always pull the latest changes to avoid conflicts.

5. **Use Branches Strategically**:
   - o Keep the main branch stable and use feature branches for development.

20.5 Advanced Git Concepts

1. **Rebasing**:
   - o Streamline a branch's commit history by moving it to a new base.

bash

```
git rebase main
```

2. **Stashing**:
   - o Save changes temporarily without committing.

bash

```
git stash
git stash apply
```

3. **Tagging**:

o Mark specific points in the repository's history, such as releases.

bash

```
git tag -a v1.0 -m "Version 1.0 release"
git push origin v1.0
```

Git is an indispensable tool for modern software development, enabling efficient collaboration and robust version control. In this chapter, you learned the basics of Git, including commit, push, pull, and branching, and applied these concepts to a real-world project. By mastering Git, you can work seamlessly on individual or team projects, maintain clean workflows, and manage codebases effectively.

In the next chapter, we'll explore **deploying applications**, where you'll learn how to prepare, package, and launch your software for production. Let's continue coding!

CHAPTER 21: TESTING AND QUALITY ASSURANCE

Testing and Quality Assurance (QA) are crucial in software development to ensure that applications work as intended, meet requirements, and are free of defects. This chapter covers:

- Writing test cases in **Python** and **Java**.
- Using unit testing frameworks: **pytest** (Python) and **JUnit** (Java).
- A real-world example: Testing a banking application.

21.1 Writing Test Cases

21.1.1 What is a Test Case?

A test case is a set of conditions or inputs used to verify that a system behaves as expected.

21.1.2 Structure of a Test Case

1. **Arrange**:
   o Set up the conditions for the test.
2. **Act**:
   o Execute the functionality to be tested.
3. **Assert**:
   o Verify that the expected and actual results match.

21.1.3 Example Test Case

Scenario: A banking application has a method deposit(amount) that adds money to an account.

Test Case:

- **Input**: Initial balance = $100, deposit = $50.
- **Expected Output**: Final balance = $150.

21.2 Unit Testing Frameworks

Unit testing involves testing individual components (functions, methods) in isolation.

21.2.1 Unit Testing in Python: *pytest*

pytest is a popular framework for writing and running Python tests.

Installation:

bash

pip install pytest

Example:

python

```
# banking_app.py
class BankAccount:
    def __init__(self, balance=0):
        self.balance = balance

    def deposit(self, amount):
        if amount < 0:
            raise ValueError("Amount must be positive")
        self.balance += amount
        return self.balance
```

```
# test_banking_app.py
import pytest
```

```python
from banking_app import BankAccount

def test_deposit():
    account = BankAccount(100)
    new_balance = account.deposit(50)
    assert new_balance == 150

def test_negative_deposit():
    account = BankAccount()
    with pytest.raises(ValueError):
        account.deposit(-10)
```

Run the Tests:

bash

pytest

Output:

css

```
test_banking_app.py ..                [100%]
2 passed in 0.02s
```

21.2.2 Unit Testing in Java: JUnit

JUnit is a widely-used framework for Java unit testing.

Setup: Add JUnit dependency to your pom.xml (Maven):

xml

```xml
<dependency>
    <groupId>org.junit.jupiter</groupId>
    <artifactId>junit-jupiter</artifactId>
    <version>5.8.1</version>
    <scope>test</scope>
</dependency>
```

Example:

java

```java
// BankAccount.java
public class BankAccount {
    private double balance;

    public BankAccount(double initialBalance) {
        this.balance = initialBalance;
    }

    public double deposit(double amount) {
        if (amount < 0) {
            throw new IllegalArgumentException("Amount must be positive");
```

```java
    }
    balance += amount;
    return balance;
  }

  public double getBalance() {
    return balance;
  }
}


// BankAccountTest.java
import org.junit.jupiter.api.Test;
import static org.junit.jupiter.api.Assertions.*;

class BankAccountTest {

  @Test
  void testDeposit() {
    BankAccount account = new BankAccount(100);
    double newBalance = account.deposit(50);
    assertEquals(150, newBalance);
  }

  @Test
  void testNegativeDeposit() {
```

```java
BankAccount account = new BankAccount(100);
Exception exception = assertThrows(IllegalArgumentException.class, () -> {
    account.deposit(-10);
});
assertEquals("Amount must be positive", exception.getMessage());
    }
}
```

Run the Tests: Use your IDE or run from the command line:

bash

mvn test

Output:

yaml

[INFO] Tests run: 2, Failures: 0, Errors: 0, Skipped: 0

21.3 Real-World Example: Testing a Banking Application

21.3.1 Problem Description

The banking application should:

1. Allow deposits and withdrawals.

2. Prevent negative deposits.

3. Prevent overdrafts during withdrawals.

21.3.2 Python Implementation

Banking Application:

python

```python
# banking_app.py
class BankAccount:
    def __init__(self, balance=0):
        self.balance = balance

    def deposit(self, amount):
        if amount < 0:
            raise ValueError("Amount must be positive")
        self.balance += amount
        return self.balance

    def withdraw(self, amount):
        if amount > self.balance:
            raise ValueError("Insufficient funds")
        self.balance -= amount
        return self.balance
```

Test Cases:

python

```python
# test_banking_app.py
import pytest
from banking_app import BankAccount

def test_deposit():
    account = BankAccount(100)
    assert account.deposit(50) == 150

def test_withdraw():
    account = BankAccount(100)
    assert account.withdraw(50) == 50

def test_negative_deposit():
    account = BankAccount()
    with pytest.raises(ValueError):
        account.deposit(-10)

def test_overdraft():
    account = BankAccount(100)
    with pytest.raises(ValueError):
        account.withdraw(200)
```

21.3.3 Java Implementation

Banking Application:

java

```java
// BankAccount.java
public class BankAccount {
    private double balance;

    public BankAccount(double initialBalance) {
        this.balance = initialBalance;
    }

    public double deposit(double amount) {
        if (amount < 0) {
            throw new IllegalArgumentException("Amount must be positive");
        }
        balance += amount;
        return balance;
    }

    public double withdraw(double amount) {
        if (amount > balance) {
            throw new IllegalArgumentException("Insufficient funds");
        }
```

```java
        balance -= amount;
        return balance;
    }

    public double getBalance() {
        return balance;
    }
}
```

Test Cases:

java

```java
// BankAccountTest.java
import org.junit.jupiter.api.Test;
import static org.junit.jupiter.api.Assertions.*;

class BankAccountTest {

    @Test
    void testDeposit() {
        BankAccount account = new BankAccount(100);
        assertEquals(150, account.deposit(50));
    }

    @Test
    void testWithdraw() {
```

```java
        BankAccount account = new BankAccount(100);
        assertEquals(50, account.withdraw(50));
    }

    @Test
    void testNegativeDeposit() {
        BankAccount account = new BankAccount(100);
        Exception                    exception                    =
assertThrows(IllegalArgumentException.class, () -> {
            account.deposit(-10);
        });
        assertEquals("Amount        must        be        positive",
exception.getMessage());
    }

    @Test
    void testOverdraft() {
        BankAccount account = new BankAccount(100);
        Exception                    exception                    =
assertThrows(IllegalArgumentException.class, () -> {
            account.withdraw(200);
        });
        assertEquals("Insufficient funds", exception.getMessage());
    }
}
```

21.4 Best Practices for Testing

1. **Test Early and Often**:
   o Write tests during development, not after.
2. **Automate Tests**:
   o Use frameworks like pytest and JUnit for consistent testing.
3. **Write Clear Test Cases**:
   o Include meaningful test names and descriptive error messages.
4. **Test Edge Cases**:
   o Handle unusual inputs and boundary conditions.
5. **Use Mocking**:
   o Simulate external dependencies during testing.
6. **Maintain Code Coverage**:
   o Aim for high test coverage to reduce bugs.

Testing ensures the reliability, security, and correctness of software applications. In this chapter, you learned how to write and run test cases in Python and Java using pytest and JUnit. You applied these techniques to a banking application, testing its core functionalities and handling edge cases. By implementing robust testing practices, you can deliver high-quality software that meets user expectations.

In the next chapter, we'll explore **application deployment**, focusing on how to prepare and launch software for production environments. Let's continue coding!

CHAPTER 22: OPTIMIZING CODE

Code optimization is the process of improving the efficiency and performance of your code by reducing its runtime, memory usage, or complexity. This chapter covers:

- The importance of code efficiency and common optimization techniques.
- Profiling tools for **Python** and **Java** to identify bottlenecks.
- A real-world example: Speeding up a data processing script.

22.1 Understanding Code Efficiency

22.1.1 What is Code Efficiency?

Code efficiency measures how well a program uses resources like time and memory to perform a task. Efficient code:

- Executes faster.
- Consumes less memory.
- Scales well with larger datasets.

22.1.2 Analyzing Algorithmic Complexity

Algorithmic complexity is expressed using **Big-O notation**, which describes how an algorithm's performance scales with input size.

Operation	Example	Complexity
Constant time	x = arr[0]	$O(1)O(1)O(1)$
Linear time	for x in arr	$O(n)O(n)O(n)$
Quadratic time	Nested loops	$O(n2)O(n^2)O(n2)$
Logarithmic time	Binary search	$O(\log n)O(\log n)O(\log n)$

Example:

- Finding the sum of a list:
  - Naive: $O(n2)O(n^2)O(n2)$ with nested loops.
  - Optimized: $O(n)O(n)O(n)$ with a single pass.

22.2 Optimization Techniques

22.2.1 General Techniques

1. **Choose Better Algorithms**:
   - Replace brute-force methods with efficient algorithms.
   - Example: Use merge sort ($O(nlogn)$ $O(n \log n)$ $O(nlogn)$)) instead of bubble sort ($O(n2)$ $O(n^2)$ $O(n2)$)).

2. **Avoid Redundant Computations**:
   - Cache or memoize results to prevent recalculating.
   - Example: Store results of expensive function calls.

3. **Reduce Loops and Iterations**:
   - Combine operations or use vectorized operations (e.g., in NumPy or Pandas).

4. **Optimize Data Structures**:
   - Use appropriate data structures like sets, dictionaries, or heaps for specific tasks.

22.2.2 Python-Specific Optimizations

1. **Use Built-In Functions**:
   - Python's built-in functions like sum() and max() are optimized in C.

python

result = sum(arr) # Faster than a custom loop

2. **Leverage Libraries**:

   o Use libraries like NumPy and Pandas for data processing.

3. **Avoid Excessive Memory Usage**:

   o Use generators (yield) instead of creating large lists.

python

```
def squares(n):
    for i in range(n):
        yield i ** 2
```

22.2.3 Java-Specific Optimizations

1. **Minimize Object Creation**:

   o Reuse objects instead of creating new ones unnecessarily.

2. **Use Efficient Collections**:

   o Use ArrayList for dynamic arrays, HashMap for key-value pairs, and PriorityQueue for heaps.

3. **Parallel Streams**:

   o Use Java 8 Streams for parallel processing:

java

numbers.parallelStream().forEach(System.out::println);

22.3 Profiling Tools

Profiling identifies performance bottlenecks by analyzing runtime and resource usage.

22.3.1 Profiling in Python

1. **cProfile**:
   - Python's built-in profiler.

   bash

   python -m cProfile script.py

2. **line_profiler**:
   - Provides line-by-line profiling.

   bash

   pip install line_profiler
   kernprof -l script.py

3. **timeit**:

- o Measures the execution time of small code snippets.

python

import timeit
print(timeit.timeit("sum(range(1000))", number=1000))

22.3.2 Profiling in Java

1. **VisualVM**:
   - o A graphical profiler for Java applications.
   - o Provides CPU and memory usage details.
2. **JProfiler**:
   - o A commercial profiler with advanced features for Java applications.
3. **Java Flight Recorder**:
   - o Built into the JVM for profiling production systems.

Usage Example: Run your Java application with profiling enabled:

bash

```
java -XX:+UnlockCommercialFeatures -XX:+FlightRecorder -jar app.jar
```

22.4 Real-World Example: Speeding Up a Data Processing Script

22.4.1 Problem Description

You have a script that processes large datasets to calculate summary statistics. The initial implementation is slow, and you need to optimize it.

22.4.2 Python Implementation
Initial Implementation:

python

```
data = [x for x in range(1000000)]

# Calculate mean
mean = sum(data) / len(data)

# Find max
max_value = max(data)

print("Mean:", mean)
print("Max:", max_value)
```

Profile with cProfile:

bash

```
python -m cProfile script.py
```

Optimization:

- Use **NumPy** for faster computations.

```python
python

import numpy as np

data = np.array([x for x in range(1000000)])

# Calculate mean and max
mean = np.mean(data)
max_value = np.max(data)

print("Mean:", mean)
print("Max:", max_value)
```

22.4.3 Java Implementation

Initial Implementation:

```java
java

import java.util.ArrayList;
import java.util.List;
```

```java
public class DataProcessing {
    public static void main(String[] args) {
        List<Integer> data = new ArrayList<>();
        for (int i = 0; i < 1000000; i++) {
            data.add(i);
        }

        // Calculate mean
        double sum = 0;
        for (int num : data) {
            sum += num;
        }
        double mean = sum / data.size();

        // Find max
        int max = data.get(0);
        for (int num : data) {
            if (num > max) {
                max = num;
            }
        }

        System.out.println("Mean: " + mean);
        System.out.println("Max: " + max);
```

```
    }

}
```

Profile with VisualVM:

1. Run the program and attach VisualVM to monitor performance.
2. Identify bottlenecks in loops.

Optimization:

- Use Java 8 Streams for parallel processing.

java

```java
import java.util.stream.IntStream;

public class OptimizedDataProcessing {
    public static void main(String[] args) {
        int[] data = IntStream.range(0, 1000000).toArray();

        // Calculate mean
        double mean = IntStream.of(data).average().orElse(0);

        // Find max
        int                    max                    =
IntStream.of(data).max().orElse(Integer.MIN_VALUE);
```

```
System.out.println("Mean: " + mean);
System.out.println("Max: " + max);
    }
}
```

22.5 Best Practices for Code Optimization

1. **Focus on Bottlenecks**:
   - Profile first to identify slow parts of the code.
2. **Use Efficient Libraries**:
   - Leverage optimized libraries (e.g., NumPy, Streams).
3. **Avoid Premature Optimization**:
   - Write clear and maintainable code first; optimize only when necessary.
4. **Minimize I/O Operations**:
   - Batch I/O operations to reduce overhead.
5. **Leverage Parallelism**:
   - Use parallel processing for computationally intensive tasks.

Optimizing code improves its efficiency, scalability, and user experience. In this chapter, you learned about analyzing algorithmic complexity, applying optimization techniques, and using profiling tools like cProfile (Python) and VisualVM (Java). Through the real-world example of speeding up a data processing script, you applied practical methods to achieve significant performance gains. With these skills, you can build high-performance software tailored to real-world demands.

In the final chapter, we'll summarize your journey through this book and provide tips for applying these skills in real-world scenarios. Let's wrap up!

CHAPTER 23: PLANNING YOUR CODING PROJECTS

Effective planning is a crucial step in successfully executing coding projects. Proper planning ensures clarity, organization, and efficient use of resources. This chapter covers:

- Breaking down tasks using **pseudocode** and **flowcharts**.
- Managing a project from start to finish with practical methodologies.
- A real-world example: Planning and executing a **personal portfolio project**.

23.1 Breaking Down Tasks

Breaking a project into smaller, manageable tasks helps you focus on each part systematically. Two essential tools for task breakdown are **pseudocode** and **flowcharts**.

23.1.1 Pseudocode

Pseudocode is a plain-language outline of your code's logic. It helps you think through the structure and functionality before implementation.

Example: A program that calculates the sum of numbers in a list.

plaintext

1. Initialize a variable to store the total sum.
2. Loop through each number in the list.
3. Add the number to the total sum.
4. Output the total sum.

Benefits:

- Easy to write and understand.
- Focuses on logic, not syntax.
- Bridges the gap between planning and coding.

23.1.2 Flowcharts

Flowcharts visually represent the flow of logic or processes in a program. They use standard symbols:

- **Oval**: Start/End.
- **Rectangle**: Process or operation.
- **Diamond**: Decision.
- **Arrow**: Flow direction.

Example: A program that checks if a number is even or odd.

plaintext

Start → Input number → Is number % 2 == 0? → Yes → Output "Even" → End

＼ No → Output "Odd" → End

23.2 Managing a Project from Start to Finish

23.2.1 Key Phases of a Project

1. **Planning**:
   - Define the project scope and goals.
   - Identify deliverables and deadlines.
2. **Designing**:
   - Create wireframes or prototypes for visual design.
   - Use pseudocode or flowcharts for logical design.
3. **Implementation**:
   - Write and test the code in small increments.
   - Regularly commit changes to version control (e.g., Git).
4. **Testing**:
   - Perform unit tests, integration tests, and user acceptance tests.
5. **Deployment**:

- o Host the project on a live server or platform (e.g., GitHub Pages, Heroku).
- o Ensure the application is stable and accessible.

6. **Maintenance**:
   - o Fix bugs and update features based on feedback.

23.2.2 Project Management Methodologies

1. **Agile**:
   - o Focuses on iterative development with frequent feedback.
   - o Suited for dynamic projects with changing requirements.

2. **Waterfall**:
   - o A linear approach with distinct phases (e.g., planning, designing, coding).
   - o Works well for well-defined, smaller projects.

3. **Kanban**:
   - o Visualizes tasks using boards (e.g., "To Do," "In Progress," "Done").
   - o Tools: Trello, Jira.

23.3 Real-World Example: Planning a Personal Portfolio Project

23.3.1 Project Goal

Create a responsive portfolio website to showcase your projects and skills.

23.3.2 Breaking Down the Project

1. **Features**:
    - o Home page: Introduction and summary.
    - o About page: Skills, education, and experience.
    - o Projects page: Showcase completed projects with descriptions.
    - o Contact page: Contact form and social media links.
2. **Pseudocode**:

plaintext

1. Initialize a project folder with HTML, CSS, and JavaScript files.
2. Create an index.html file for the home page.
3. Add navigation links for About, Projects, and Contact pages.
4. Use CSS to style the layout and add responsiveness.
5. Write JavaScript for interactive features (e.g., form validation).
6. Test each page for layout and functionality.

7. Deploy the project on GitHub Pages or Netlify.

3. **Flowchart**:

plaintext

Start → Display Home Page → User clicks navigation link →
→ About Page | Projects Page | Contact Page → End

23.3.3 Managing the Project

1. **Planning**:
   - **Tools**: Google Docs (for feature list), Trello (for task management).
   - Define a timeline: 2 weeks for design, 1 week for coding, 1 week for testing and deployment.
2. **Designing**:
   - Create wireframes using Figma or Adobe XD.
   - Sketch the structure of each page.
3. **Implementation**:
   - **Tools**: VS Code, Git.
   - Write code incrementally:
     - HTML structure → CSS styling → JavaScript interactivity.
4. **Testing**:
   - Test responsiveness on different screen sizes.

o Use tools like Lighthouse for performance and accessibility checks.

5. **Deployment**:

o Push the code to GitHub.

o Deploy using GitHub Pages or Netlify.

23.3.4 Tools and Technologies

1. **Development**:

o **Languages**: HTML, CSS, JavaScript.

o **Frameworks**: Bootstrap for faster styling.

2. **Version Control**:

o **Git**: Track changes and collaborate (if working with others).

3. **Deployment**:

o **GitHub Pages**: Host static websites for free.

o **Netlify**: Free hosting with continuous integration.

23.4 Best Practices for Project Planning

1. **Define Clear Goals**:

o Ensure all team members understand the project's purpose.

2. **Use Milestones**:

   o   Break the project into achievable phases.

3. **Track Progress**:

   o   Regularly update tasks in project management tools.

4. **Iterate and Improve**:

   o   Review progress and make adjustments as needed.

5. **Document Everything**:

   o   Maintain detailed documentation for the code and project workflow.

Planning is a critical step in ensuring coding projects are well-organized, efficient, and successful. This chapter taught you how to break down tasks with pseudocode and flowcharts, manage a project through its lifecycle, and apply these concepts to a real-world portfolio project. By adopting best practices and leveraging appropriate tools, you can execute projects with confidence and deliver impactful results.

In the final chapter, we'll summarize key takeaways from the book and outline strategies for applying these skills in real-world coding scenarios. Let's finish strong!

www.ingramcontent.com/pod-product-compliance
Lightning Source LLC
LaVergne TN
LVHW022338060326
832902LV00022B/4118